002029   1950

TWO HUNGRY GIANTS

Written under the auspices
of the Center for International Affairs,
Harvard University

Two Hungry Giants

The United States and Japan in the
Quest for Oil and Ores

RAYMOND VERNON

Harvard University Press
Cambridge, Massachusetts
and London, England 1983

This book is printed on acid-free paper,
and its binding materials have been chosen
for strength and durability.

Library of Congress Cataloging in Publication Data

Vernon, Raymond, 1913-
    Two hungry giants.

    "Written under the auspices of the Center for Inter-
national Affairs, Harvard University"—P.
    Includes bibliographical references and index.
    1. United States—Foreign economic relations—Japan.
2. Japan—Foreign economic relations—United States.
3. Raw materials. 4. Competition, International.
I. Harvard University. Center for International Affairs.
II. Title.
HF1456.5.J3V47 1983   382'.42'0952   82-15525
ISBN 0-674-91470-8

PREFACE

I first set foot on Japanese soil on January 1, 1946, stepping out from a DC-4 onto the Haneda airstrip at the edge of Sagami Sea. I was one of a band of eight wide-eyed Americans bent on a quixotic task, that of developing a program to restructure Japan's great industrial combines, the so-called *zaibatsu*. Our innocence and our ignorance were both of monumental proportions, a fact that we soon recognized. This was the beginning of my fascination — now common enough among Americans — with the complex, subtle, frustratingly contradictory culture that the Japanese had developed over centuries of separateness on their little archipelago. In the decades following, I found myself constantly looking for opportunities to satisfy an intense curiosity about the country, its language, its culture, and its people.

This study was propelled as much by my hunger to learn more about Japan as by any other factor. An unexpected dividend has been the insights the study has provided about the behavior of another great industrial power, the United States. Two countries could not have responded more differently to a similar problem. And in each case, with startling consistency, the responses seemed to stem from the distinctive aspects of each country's history and culture, almost as if the country had no choice but to pursue the policies it selected. In this respect, the study has had a sobering effect. It suggests that, in this field of policy at any rate, national leaders have been prisoners of their national environment, perhaps much more than they have been prepared to recognize.

My guess is that the field of policy covered here is representative of a much wider policy area — namely, the whole range of international issues that affect domestic economies in a direct and immediate way. Those of us whose vocation entails analyzing, second guessing, and occasionally advising national leaders who pretend to be making foreign policy in such areas need to understand much more thoroughly the nature of these restraints. As long as the world's space continues to be divided so incongruously among the fractious, in-turned, self-concerned sovereigns that now occupy it, learning how to deal with these national restraints may prove to be the most important challenge in the critical job of improving international relations. That is the spirit in which this analysis is presented.

The study itself was a team effort, financed on a shoestring mainly from the slim resources of the U.S.-Japan Program of the Center for International Affairs. There was also a small gift from Pfizer, Inc., as well as the contributions eked out from various student aid funds, including notably the Federal Work Study Program.

My mainstays in the work were five graduate students: James Brenner, Mark Brown, Mia de Kuijper, Brian Levy, and Dani Rodrik; Levy played a special role, as coworker and junior colleague. Some of these have since published independent articles on the basis of the work they contributed to the group. In addition, there was a supply of indefatigable research assistants who burrowed for endless hours in libraries and data banks to test my hypotheses and recollections. These included Steven Baral, Marie Chandoha, Marybeth Deily, Jack Dulberger, Terry L. Hansen, Jr., Olga B. Jonas, Nancy Kerrebrock, Eileen M. Mullen, James Murchie, and Steven Pollock. Finally, there were a number of Japanese friends and colleagues associated with the U.S.-Japan Program of the Center for International Affairs who challenged some of my more reckless hypotheses with polite expressions of slight doubt, steered me to new sources of data, and otherwise kept me on the straight and narrow; Munemichi Inoue, Hisao Mitsuyu and Hiroshi Yokokawa were particularly assiduous in this role. As usual, Josephine Vernon went meticulously through the text, ferreting out errors, ambiguities, and false notes. Ezra Vogel and Louis T. Wells, Jr., generously read portions of the manuscript and guided me on various issues.

The preparation of this manuscript was in the able hands of Andrée Brown, who learned to coax new miracles out of the word processor in a succession of triumphs over deadlines.

CONTENTS

TWO HUNGRY GIANTS

1
PARTNERS
OR
RIVALS

In the modern history of international relations, the struggles of industrial states over the control of basic raw materials have provided a recurrent theme.[1] The urge of industrialized nations to capture secure sources of raw materials was a major factor in the competition among European powers as they carved up Africa during the last decades of the nineteenth century; it figured in the motives of Germany and Japan in the great wars of the twentieth century; it pitted Britain, France, and the United States against one another during the 1920s in arcane political maneuvers over the Middle East; and it occupied center stage in the 1970s as the members of the Organization of Petroleum Exporting Countries (OPEC) attempted to control the world market for oil.

At first glance, the problems that industrial nations face today in acquiring secure sources of raw materials may seem more acute — and the likelihood of friction greater — than ever before. Until a few decades ago, the leading industrial power of the West, the United States, was fairly secure with respect to its supplies of critical raw materials (see Appendix, Table 1); but today it is heavily dependent on the importation of such materials. At the same time, the economy of Japan, which has always lacked secure access to a supply of materials, has grown from a midget to a giant. In the past quarter-century, for instance, Japan's consumption of energy in various forms has increased about sevenfold and its production of steel more than fifteenfold.

The result is that the needs of the United States and Japan have come to dominate the world's raw material markets. In 1979 the two countries consumed 46 percent of the world's crude oil outside the communist countries, 39 percent of the world's bauxite and alumina, 53 percent of its iron ore, 36 percent of its copper, and 46 percent of its coal (see Appendix, Table 2). When measured by their role in the international trade in industrial raw materials, rather than by their consumption, the joint position of these two countries is likewise prominent. Their imports of crude oil accounted for 39 percent of the world's imports of that critical material, while their imports of bauxite, alumina, iron ore, copper, and coal ran between 31 and 78 percent of world imports. With regard to the lesser nonferrous ores, such as lead, zinc, manganese, and the like, the joint position of the United States and Japan as the world's dominant users is about as important.

By concentrating on oil and oil products, iron ore, bauxite, and copper ore, there is always a risk that we may be overlooking some critical problems that could arise in other commodities. Chromite and manganese, for instance, have always been a source of concern to U.S. strategic planners because of the concentration of their production in the Soviet Union and southern Africa. The mention of uranium never fails to evoke overtones of tension because of its special uses and its history of cartelization and restriction. The international timber trade and coal trade are never wholly free of problems affecting the two countries. In terms of sheer quantity, however, the products that are considered here represent the lion's share of the industrial raw material imports of the United States and Japan. And as the analysis develops, it will be apparent that the central generalizations of the study can be applied without great risk to other products as well.

The common dependence of these two giant economies on a set of vitally important raw materials suggests rich possibilities — for both conflict and cooperation. So far, a little of each has occurred. Japanese and U.S. firms are involved in a number of joint ventures in oil refineries in Japan, and in mining undertakings in Australia and the United States. Japan saw itself as the victim when the U.S. government enacted a prohibition on the export of Alaskan oil in 1970, and U.S. authorities were greatly exercised when Japanese firms pushed up the spot price of Middle East oil in 1979 in a scramble for scarce supplies. On the whole, however, bearing in mind the critical importance of industrial raw materials, the postwar relations of the two countries on that delicate subject have appeared remarkably unruffled.

This fact should be reassuring in itself. But the dominance of the two countries in world markets in some of these materials is of such recent vintage that past experience may be no sure guide to the future. Besides, other fundamental changes have been taking place in the positions of the two countries. Both, for instance, see their economic positions in the world economy quite differently from the way they did a decade or two ago, a fact that has been influencing their bilateral relationship substantially and promises to affect that relationship even more profoundly in the future.

The Economic Context

Guardian and ward. Thirty years ago it would have been inconceivable for Japan, in the acquisition of its raw materials, to follow a policy that risked offending the United States. At that time, the relationship between the United States and Japan was dominated by the successful ending of a seven-year, strangely benign military occupation. The occupying forces, led by Americans, operated with the ambiguity that is so commonly encountered in U.S. political behavior. Until 1948 those policies expressed themselves in various reformist programs, such as the dissolution of large holding companies (known as *zaibatsu*), the creation of an independent labor movement, and the reform of the agricultural landholding systems; after 1948, as part of the cold war strategy of the period, occupation policies concentrated on rebuilding Japan as a critical link in the containment of the Soviet Union.[2]

As a ward of the United States, Japan operated more or less contentedly in the shelter of its political and economic protection. The relative economic strength of the two parties — at the time, the U.S. gross national product was about twenty times that of Japan — helped cement those attitudes. So, too, did the global role of the United States, that of the acknowledged leader of a coalition of market economies engaged in reconstructing an open system of trade and payments.

The ups and downs in the economic relationships of the two countries during the three decades that followed have already been chronicled and dissected in a number of studies, and there is no need to deal with them here in detail.[3] Overall, they paint a picture that is strikingly consistent with the ward-guardian metaphor — including, in the end, the inevitable signs that the ward was growing up.

In the beginning, in the early 1950s, the principal role of the United States was to sponsor Japan's return as a member in good standing of the world trading system by supporting the country's bid for membership in the General Agreement on Tariff and Trade (GATT) and in other international bodies. (Much later, in 1964, the United States would be performing the same sponsoring role in securing Japanese membership in the rich countries' club, the Organization for Economic Cooperation and Development.) At that early stage, given the relative sizes and states of the two countries, the stakes in maintaining a harmonious relationship between them were far more important for Japan than they were for the United States. At the same time, Japan could hardly be pictured as a rival. Because of the relatively debilitated state of the Japanese industrial structure, U.S. policy makers refused to become greatly concerned about the threat of Japanese competition in U.S. markets. And as long as Japan was short of foreign exchange, U.S. officials were prepared to accept the tight system of trade controls and foreign exchange controls that the Japanese government was imposing.

But not for long. By the mid-1950s, the ward was already exhibiting an unanticipated and disconcerting capacity for creating difficulties for its guardian. These early manifestations of Japanese competitive capabilities were only marginally threatening to the U.S. economy, inasmuch as they were mainly centered on cotton textiles and related price-elastic soft goods. A decade or two later, when automobiles and semiconductors were to be at the heart of the bilateral competition, the threat to the U.S. economy would be seen as much more severe. But with pressure-group politics playing so important a role in the U.S. process, neither the Republican administration of the 1950s nor the Democratic administration of President Kennedy felt safe in disregarding the issue. So cotton textile imports were elevated to a problem of seemingly major importance between the two countries.

On the U.S. side, some officials saw the problem as irritating because it had been created by the unexpectedly vigorous and effective behavior of a sheltered ward. It was all the more irritating because any effective U.S. response appeared to be so costly. In general, the U.S. system of trade controls was quite open and nondiscriminatory. There were extensive restrictions on agricultural imports, to be sure; but these were tolerated under the rules of the General Agreement on Tariffs and Trade. And although there were the beginnings of a system of restrictions on crude oil, oil was always looked on as a special product, not subject to the usual rules of the game. Unlike the Japanese, the Americans maintained no general system of import restrictions or foreign exchange controls. The U.S. leadership role in the GATT would be compromised if the United States were to adopt a new set of import restrictions — discriminatory restrictions, at that — aimed at Japanese cotton textiles.

To U.S. policy makers of the period, the problem was relatively simple: to find some course of action that dealt with this irritating political problem, without greatly compromising the U.S. international position. The obvious solution was to have the Japanese accommodate American needs by imposing "voluntary" restrictions on their exports of cotton textiles.

Accordingly, in 1956 the Americans began putting pressure on the Japanese. A law was enacted that empowered the president to negotiate agreements limiting exports of textiles from foreign countries and that authorized him to restrict the importation of such products on an emergency basis. By 1957 Japan had "voluntarily" adopted a five-year program of export controls.[4]

For the Japanese, the American demands were the first of a series of *shokus* (shocks) that would occur repeatedly, and apparently with almost undiminished impact, over the next ten or fifteen years. Playing the role of ward, the Japanese had become completely committed to the part. Lacking raw materials and bereft of the economic power to negotiate for entry into foreign markets, they had accepted the proffered guardianship of the United States and had turned uninhibitedly to the task of rebuilding their economy. Relying on their high internal rate of savings for capital, they reached out systematically for foreign technology to put the capital to work. With draconian controls, foreign inputs were held down mainly to indispensable raw materials and technology; and with hard work, exports were built up rapidly to remarkably high levels.

During the 1960s the ward-guardian relationship began to wear thin, at least where issues of industry and trade were involved. By the early part of the decade it was beginning to be clear to businessmen and officials in the United States and elsewhere that Japan could prove a formidable competitor. For the Japanese themselves, however, a change in perception of the country's position was understandably slower in coming. Other countries began to demand of Japan that it should open up its markets for their goods; pressures of this sort kept mounting in the meetings of the GATT and the International Monetary Fund, as well as through bilateral diplomatic channels. Moreover, businessmen and officials in some countries—especially in the United States—found it incomprehensible, or else saw it as a mark of ingratitude, that the Japanese should be preventing U.S.-based enterprises from setting up subsidiaries on Japanese soil.

On the Japanese side, the great economic successes of the 1960s were accompanied by disconcerting consequences.[5] Some countries had never been wholly reconciled to admitting Japan to full membership in the GATT; indeed, a number of signatories of that agreement had exercised their right, at the time of Japan's accession, not to apply the GATT's provisions to that country. Special restrictions on Japanese goods persisted and multiplied. And as Japan's exports broadened, the American government extracted more "voluntary" restraints from Japanese exporters. European governments followed suit with much less ambivalence and with much more effect, adding a series of overt and not-so-overt techniques for augmenting the effects of the negotiated "voluntary" restrictions.

Toward the close of the 1960s, acrimonious debates between the United States and Japan served notice to the Japanese that they could no longer hope to play the role of American ward, at least not in matters of trade and investment. In a succession of incidents, the U.S. president and the Japanese prime minister found themselves in angry confrontation.[6] Nixon's efforts to persuade Sato to restrict Japan's textile exports became deeply entangled in Japanese and U.S. politics, leading to charges and countercharges of bad faith. Nixon next resumed diplomatic ties with the People's Republic of China. The fact that Japan's government was not consulted in advance was viewed as an extraordinary slight by the Japanese. These events were followed in the summer of 1971 by the suspension of convertibility of the U.S. dollar along with the temporary imposition of a surcharge on U.S. imports. For Japan, the guardian's mantle had been withdrawn.

The guardian's retreat. As long as the guardian-ward relationship prevailed, the relative roles of the two countries were reasonably well defined. Although disagreements might arise between them, the role of the United States was to provide the security umbrella and to maintain the open world trading system that were essential for Japan's well-being. And the role of Japan, in the end, was to cultivate the good graces of the United States and to maintain their alliance in working order.

Gradually, however, it was becoming evident that the roles of the two countries were changing.[7] The desire of the United States to keep the doors open for Japanese goods in world markets was melting away. Even if the desire had remained, the leadership role of the United States in the GATT was becoming increasingly equivocal.

Part of the reason for this change in leadership position was a shift in U.S. perceptions. During the first decade after the end of World War II, the Americans viewed themselves as the free world's undisputed leader, responsible for developing and sustaining a global trading system. But in the two decades following, that sense of leadership became more narrowly confined to questions of military security. The change in perception was accompanied by a decline in the country's relative economic weight. In 1950 the gross national product of the United States constituted about 62 percent of the product of all the countries that now make up the membership of the Organization for Economic Cooperation and Development (OECD); by 1970 that ratio was down to 48 percent. In 1950 U.S. exports amounted to about 50 percent of the exports of the group; by 1970 that ratio had dropped to 19 percent. Moreover, by 1970 the competitive capabilities of the U.S. economy were being strongly questioned. Accordingly, in the early 1970s, as the United States and other countries prepared for another giant GATT tariff negotiation, it grew clear that neither the United States itself nor the other principal members of the GATT took U.S. leadership quite as much for granted as in the past.

As the Japanese began to realize that they were on their own, the government began seriously to liberalize its pervasive restrictions on trade and investment, hoping to fortify its acceptance by other countries.[8] That step came hard, pushing against the nation's cultural preferences and historical precedents. Nevertheless, during the 1970s Japan gradually dismantled its elaborate structure of restrictions on trade and investment.[9] By 1982 the level of its tariffs was one of the world's lowest. More important, the government was engaged in an ambitious process of dredging out some deeply embedded barriers to importation that lay outside its tariff structure and its foreign exchange licensing system. The manifold devices that had served to exclude foreign goods for so long were being systematically reviewed and revised; the elaborate inspection schemes, the meticulous classification systems, the forbidding standards purporting to be based on health and safety requirements, the import cartels, and so on seemed to be going through a process of modification that might eventually bring them closer to the norms of other industrialized countries.[10]

Ironically, at the very time that Japan was persuading itself to liberalize its various measures for restricting imports, the rest of the world was becoming increasingly eclectic about the kind of arrangements that were acceptable in international trade. Particularly apparent was an increasing tolerance for discriminatory trading arrangements, a tolerance that would eventually have considerable bearing on the structure of the world's raw material markets.

The first signs of such tolerance had, in fact, appeared long before the 1970s, but at first they had been fairly well contained within defined limits. The U.S. government's occasional use of "voluntary" export agreements, such as those imposed on Japan in 1956, were exceptional in their time. But they proved a forerunner of more to come. Such agreements proliferated in the decades that followed. By 1965 a multilateral Multifibers Agreement was concluded, which was intended both to legitimate and to restrain these coercive bilateral accords. The agreement legitimated the accords but did very little to restrain them,[11] and by the early 1980s such accords had become embedded in the trade controls of nearly all industrialized countries.

During the 1960s and 1970s, the movement away from the GATT's nondiscriminatory norms was taking place on other fronts as well. The European Economic Community (EEC), exempted from the GATT's principle of nondiscrimination because it was defined as a customs union, proved to be the nucleus of a broad network of discriminatory arrangements. The EEC created a series of free-trade arrangements with the member governments of the European Free Trade Association, a succession of bilateral preferential agreements with individual countries in the Mediterranean basin, and a convention extending preferential trading rights to some sixty developing countries located in Africa, the Caribbean area, and the Pacific.[12] Moreover, members of the GATT that could qualify as developing countries, operating under special provisions of the agreement, were allowed to experiment with an unending variety of preferential trade arrangements among themselves, ranging from elaborate free-trade areas to limited discriminatory bilateral agreements.[13]

By the early 1980s, these various discriminatory trade arrangements were being augmented by the growth of trade from the centrally directed economies of Eastern Europe and Asia—that is, the Soviet Union, China, and the Eastern European states. In 1960 the exports of these countries to the noncommunist world had amounted to only 2.9 percent of the world's exports; but by 1980 the figure was above 5 percent. Industrial raw materials, including mineral ores, oil, and coal, had always had a prominent place in such trade. And they promised to have an even greater role in the future, as the U.S.S.R. planned to ship large quantities of gas to Western Europe and as the People's Republic of China planned to expand its exports of oil, coal, and other materials into world markets. Wherever the centrally directed economies could arrange to do so, they strongly preferred to enter into bilateral agreements with the governments of other countries, agreements that in practice proved inescapably discriminatory against the goods of third countries. Even where government-to-government agreements could not be arranged, the Soviet Union, China, and the others sought to balance their trade in deals with individual firms, using various modified forms of barter for the purpose.[14] But despite these obvious discriminatory actions, the members of the GATT could not bring themselves to face the issue.

The growing tendency of members of international organizations to tolerate discriminatory practices has gone hand in hand with a growing tendency of the United States to declare its readiness to engage in such practices. The latter may well be a reflection of the fact that the American public today sees the U.S. role in international affairs in terms quite different from those that would have been encountered a decade or two earlier. The change, however, cannot be described in simple isolationist-internationalist political terms or in protectionist-globalist economic terms. The recognition by Americans that the political and economic interests of the country are linked to those of many foreign countries is undiminished; indeed, it may even have acquired greater strength over the years. But there appears to be a greater reluctance to think in terms of global systems for dealing with global problems, and an increased preference for an eclectic and selective approach to international issues.[15]

In any event, those concerned with the future behavior of the U.S. government in the acquisition of industrial raw materials could not begin with quite so strong a presumption as in years past that U.S.

policies would be generally nondiscriminatory in their structure. Already in 1974, when the U.S. Congress renewed the president's power to negotiate for the reduction of U.S. tariffs, its authorization carried a number of important provisions contemplating the possibility of discriminatory trade practices. Perhaps the most important in principle was Section 301 of the Trade Act of 1974, a provision that went to some lengths to authorize the president to retaliate against any country that he might find engaging in "unfair trade practices" against the United States. Subsequently, when the U.S. delegation brought home various codes on the application of nontariff barriers that had been negotiated among members of the GATT, the Congress carefully provided that any rights extended to other countries pursuant to such codes — such as the right to sell goods to government agencies — should be limited only to the signatories of such codes, thereby exposing members of the GATT who had not signed the codes to discriminatory treatment.[16] In fact, almost immediately after the codes were ratified by the Congress, U.S. and Japanese representatives set about discussing how the code on government procurement might be applied in trade between them; that discussion elaborated the special provisions of the code.[17]

A telling manifestation of increased U.S. willingness to play with the idea of discriminatory trade arrangements was the widespread public discussion in the latter 1970s of a North American energy market, as well as the proposal of the Reagan administration to develop a preferential trading arrangement with selected countries in the Caribbean area.[18] The idea of a preferential area, while not totally without precedent in U.S. history, represented a rare departure from the national policy of nondiscrimination. Yet that aspect of the proposal barely evoked comment; subsequent resistance was centered almost exclusively on the proposal's threat to individual U.S. industries, rather on its discriminatory character.[19]

Of even greater significance is the widespread tendency of public officials to give equal weight to "reciprocity" and "fair trade" as formal principles for the conduct of U.S. trade relations.[20] "Reciprocity" has become a code word with a special meaning: the United States would treat each country in any economic transaction according to the country's treatment of the United States in that kind of transaction. The concept is, of course, indistinguishable from a bilateral discriminatory approach. In 1982 Congress considered perhaps twenty different bills that would embody this principle in U.S. trade policies. In light of its long traditions, the United States can be expected to pause a little before it explicitly accepts a discriminatory approach as a major element in the conduct of international trade relations. But the strong tilt in that direction in the early 1980s was fairly evident.

The era of interdependence. If the roles of guardian and ward helped explain the interaction between the United States and Japan in the 1950s, the ties of interdependence help explain the interaction between them in the 1980s. Part of that interdependence has been the result of the importance that each country attached to the other in building its security. But part could be ascribed to a worldwide trend that has been increasing the economic links between practically all national economies.

In the decades after World War II, most nations found that their ties to foreign economies were growing in number and diversity. As the technological improvements in transportation and communication made their mark and as the U.S.-led open trading system reduced existing trade barriers, the economic structures of the industrialized economies grew increasingly interrelated. From 1963 to 1973, for instance, the world's exports of manufactures grew at the extraordinary rate of 11 percent annually in real terms, while the world's total output grew annually at only 7 percent. From 1973 to 1980, both exports and output of manufactures grew more slowly, but the margin by which export growth exceeded output growth persisted: exports grew at 5 percent, while output grew at 3.5 percent.[21]

In the course of this growth, all countries found themselves attaching increased importance to their export trade. For the Japanese this emphasis was nothing new, but for the United States the growing emphasis on exports was a novel experience. Over many decades, U.S. exports of merchandise had represented only a small part of U.S. output: in 1950, for example, such exports constituted only 6.4 percent of the country's final merchandise sales. But by 1970 the figure had risen to 9.0 percent, and by 1980 to an astonishing 19.7 percent.

As their foreign trade grew, Japan and the United States found themselves attaching considerable importance to each other's markets. In 1979 the Japanese were selling 24 percent of their exports to the U.S. market alone, while the Americans were selling 12 percent of their exports to the Japanese market. What may be even more relevant, given the nature of the U.S. political process, is that about 15 percent of U.S.

agricultural exports went to Japan, with the strong promise of more to come in the future.

The links between the various national economies of the world have been strengthened not only by the growth of international trade but also by the rapid multinational spread of national enterprises. As international communication links improved, patterns of consumption and techniques of production began to lose their distinctive national characteristics; tastes and technologies all around the world began to move toward common norms.[22] That tendency created a base for some multinational enterprises to spread their activities more broadly around the world. Because of the spread of such enterprises, a considerable part of the world's trade, on the order of one-quarter of the total, has come to consist of the transfer of goods among affiliated units of a single enterprise.[23] At the same time, international banking has undergone a significant transformation: to stay in the running, large banks are now obliged to deliver their services all over the world.

These globalizing trends, of course, have not been universal. Indeed, in the oil industry and in some of the mineral industries explored at length in this study, many long-standing multinational links were broken during the 1970s. And some of the key questions surrounding the future of the raw material industries, as we shall presently see, concerned whether these industries would acquire a new global structure, and what position multinational enterprises would have in such a structure.

The question is particularly important for the United States and Japan because of the great importance that multinational links have ordinarily played in U.S. business. By 1977 the employees of the foreign affiliates of U.S.-based enterprises had come to equal 38 percent of the number employed by these enterprises in the United States.[24] For a time after World War II, the development of multinational enterprises, including international banks, had been widely regarded as a peculiarly American phenomenon. When businesses in other countries, such as Japan, created subsidiaries in foreign countries, scholars sometimes felt moved to try to distinguish their motivations from that of U.S. firms.[25] By the early 1980s, however, the multinationalizing trend was widely recognized as similar in nature, irrespective of the nationality of the parent firm.[26] By then, the push to a multinational structure could be readily detected even among firms in the developing countries.[27]

To be sure, as far as Japan was concerned, the links that were being created by the growth of multinational enterprises had not yet become very strong. For a long time, the Japanese government had maintained effective controls over its own firms in establishing overseas subsidiaries in Japan; it was only in the 1970s that such restraints were substantially relaxed. Accordingly, even as late as 1978, foreign-owned manufacturing firms in Japan accounted for only about 4 percent of the assets of all manufacturing firms in Japan, and one-third of those foreign assets were concentrated in the oil refinery industry.[28] For its part, Japan's industry had invested only $834 million in U.S. manufacturing industry by the end of 1980, a magnitude that could barely be detected in the U.S. manufacturing aggregates.[29] Nevertheless, by the early 1980s more numerous contacts between firms that carried the flags of the two countries seemed likely. There were the usual possibilities of increased rivalry or increased cooperation in acquiring oil or minerals, as well as the possibilities of increased rivalry in the sale of finished products that used these raw materials.

The prospect of frequent contacts between the enterprises of the two countries also suggested that negotiations between the two governments on economic issues might be even more extensive than in the past. In all such contacts, Japan could be counted on to be a tough and resolute bargainer, reflecting its greatly augmented economic strength. From the viewpoint of American negotiators, of course, Japan has always been a difficult negotiator; the prospect of continued resoluteness on the part of the Japanese would be seen as nothing new. The Japanese, however, have viewed their interactions with the United States as an endless string of capitulations under pressure, prefaced by short periods of grumbling and footdragging. Expressing a view common in Japan, the retired editor-in-chief of *Business Japan* observed "The U.S. has shown in trade disputes in the past that it will forcefully impose its view, even when knowing fully well that it was being unreasonable.[30]

Not surprisingly, therefore, Japanese leaders have engaged in a certain amount of introspection over their style in future negotiations. In terms of the metaphor popular in Japanese discussions, the question has been whether Japan should pursue the style of the resolute samurai, the swift-footed merchant, or the grumbling clerk.[31] Whatever the outcome of that debate, it signals the likelihood of a more aggressive style of negotiation on the part of the Japanese.

The Security Context

The ties that link the United States to Japan are not all economic — there is a security dimension as well. And if the signs are being correctly interpreted, the security dimension may prove of increasing importance in determining how the two countries negotiate matters involving industrial raw materials.

Lenin was, of course, right when he observed that the capitalist countries associated their control over raw materials with their capacity to make war. In the case of Japan, the historical link between its acute need for raw materials and its various invasions of the Asian mainland has always been clear. In the case of the United States, the sporadic worries of the official establishment over shortages of raw materials have usually been linked to planning for war. To be sure, in the early 1980s one could have made a case that the link between war-making capacity and raw materials availability was weaker than it had been, that modern warfare depended much more heavily than in the past on the state of the military forces at the outbreak of hostilities. But from long tradition and understandable caution, military planners still would link the issues closely.

U.S. security interests were linked to Japan not only by the two countries' dependence on some key raw materials but also by their common contributions to a pool of relevant technology. By the early 1980s, U.S. military planners had developed a considerable respect for Japan's technological capabilities, especially in fiber optics and communications, and were trying to gain access to those capabilities through licensing and imports.[32]

In the early 1980s, the security orientation of Japan in relation to the United States was not easy to define. In the short run, the Soviet Union was Japan's largest source of security concern. Japan obviously had a very limited capability for defending itself against the Soviet Union, and was relying primarily on the U.S. nuclear umbrella as a deterrent. Japan was prepared to undertake some specific roles and missions in that connection, provided they were unequivocally "defensive" in character. In other respects, however, the security relationship between Japan and the United States was swathed in ambiguity.[33]

One source of the ambiguity was the fact that a large gap existed between U.S. views of the security role that Japan should play and the views of the Japanese themselves. It was becoming increasingly apparent that the objective of the U.S. military establishment was to enlist Japan as a full-fledged member of an anticommunist military alliance.[34] But despite Japan's concern over the long-run intentions of the Soviet Union, the country's leaders were far from ready to enter into the alliance desired by the Americans. Throughout most of their national history, the Japanese have exhibited an especially strong sense of their national identity, a firm view of their distinctiveness from other cultures, and a great sensitivity to the foreignness of non-Japanese cultures.[35] Japan's increasing unwillingness to be seen as a totally compliant member of the U.S. team was strengthened by the widespread feeling in Japan that the U.S. position in world affairs was being eroded, as well by the view of many Japanese that the U.S. preoccupation with the Soviet Union was exaggerated or misguided.[36]

Japan's view of its own distinctiveness has been strengthened by the fact that it was long ago assigned and long ago accepted a unique role in military affairs. At the demand of its conquerors after World War II, Japan adopted a constitution that forever denied it the right to arm. And by its own subsequent decision, Japan denied itself the right to procure, produce, or permit the introduction of nuclear weapons on Japanese soil. From the viewpoint of most Japanese, that set of half-imposed decisions has been a disguised blessing, limiting the country's responsibilities to act in support of its own security.

Nevertheless, under persistent U.S. urging, Japan has managed to build up a set of so-called Self-Defense Forces which are designed to respond to some limited objectives, such as protecting Japan's air space and sea lanes within a thousand-mile radius.[37] Japan has also arranged to provide a vast staging area for the U.S. Navy and U.S. Air Force: nearly 50,000 U.S. military personnel, 118 U.S. military facilities, and two battle-ready U.S. air wings are established in the country. Those acts have sharpened the contradiction between the country's pacifist preferences and its actual role.

Japan's uncertainties about its defense position have found expression in various forms. In response to U.S. requests for the exportation of some of the new Japanese technologies that have military implications, for instance, the government simply put off a decision for as long as possible. Behind that delay, no doubt, have been concerns that U.S. commercial interests might gain access to the technology; but Japan has also been eager not to get into the business of exporting military equipment, lest the country impair its image as a disarmed peace-loving nation.[38] For similar reasons, the Japanese government has been reluctant to give up the ceiling that it has maintained on defense expenditures, a sum not to exceed 1 percent of its gross national product.

Wrestling with the contradictions in its security policies, Japanese leaders have toyed with various theories of the special nature of the Japanese state.[39] One persistent strand in Japanese thinking has been the idea that Japan's contribution to its security and to that of its allies could take place through channels broader and more "comprehensive" than military channels alone: acting as a middleman for the West, Japan could strengthen the performance of the developing countries, improve the world's access to Persian Gulf oil, and elevate the technological achievements of all nations, while leaving the global military tasks to the United States.[40] Many Japanese feel that such a role would be more in accord with Japan's self-interest and self-perception than would an enlarged military role.

To all this introspection and rumination, the official U.S. establishment has carefully turned a blind eye. Officially, Japan has been dealt with as if it were a Pacific ally whose security interests coincided to a very considerable degree with those of the United States. Although U.S. leaders have been aware of the gap between the perceptions of the two countries regarding the security role of Japan, they have preferred — no doubt wisely — to leave the existing ambiguity undisturbed.

Another source of ambiguity in the security relationship between the United States and Japan comes from the U.S. side. That source has been generated by the swift changes that have been taking place in the system of security alliances which link the noncommunist countries, epitomized in the Atlantic alliance and the North Atlantic Treaty Organization (NATO).

In the late 1970s, numerous disputes were building up within the alliance. Those differences grew more intense with the resumption of cold war tactics by the Reagan administration. As the disputes have developed, they have come to entail some of the most fundamental questions of the nature of the Atlantic alliance and of the strategies it should pursue: to what extent the alliance should concert on strategic issues involving the Soviet Union that arise in theaters outside the Atlantic area, such as Afghanistan, Africa, and the Falkland Islands; to what extent trade and finance should be used by the alliance as instruments to persuade or coerce the Soviet Union; to what extent nuclear weapons should play a role in the defense of Western Europe;

and so on. For almost the first time, it has been Germany, not France, that has been playing the role of the leading dissident from U.S. views. Unlike the United States, Germany has been eager to expand its trade ties with Eastern Europe and the U.S.S.R., and avoid building up cold war tensions by increasing the stock of nuclear weapons in Western Europe; but at the same time, Germany has been determined to avoid any major modifications in NATO's agreed military strategy for meeting a Soviet attack, particularly modifications that would have the NATO troops pull back across Germany in the face of such an attack. In its dissident role, Germany has been getting considerable support from powerful elements in other countries.[41]

Not that the alliance's earlier history had been one of uninterrupted harmony. In 1954 there had been the defeat by France of a project for a European Defense Force, in 1956 a veto by the United States of the British-French-Israeli attack on Egypt, and in 1962 a rejection by Europe of the U.S. proposal for a multilateral naval force. In the latter 1960s a gulf had been created within the alliance by the U.S. involvement in Vietnam. The 1970s, too, had seen the fiasco over the deployment of a neutron bomb in Europe and the estrangement of the United States from its allies over its policies toward Israel.

By the early 1980s, however, it was widely assumed that the atmosphere in which the NATO alliance had been operating over the three prior decades was undergoing a sea change. Although Western Europe still displayed no strong signs of developing a security policy that was independent of the United States, the quality of its resistance to U.S. policies seemed to many observers to be different from that of earlier periods. At the same time, both the capacity and the willingness of the United States to lead the alliance seemed reduced, partly because of the relative shrinkage in the size of the U.S. economy and partly because of America's increasing impatience with Europe's insistence on an independent approach.

At issue in the minds of American planners, politicians, and scholars was the question of whether the Atlantic alliance could be expected to retain its original orientation, in which the United States footed the lion's share of the bill and exercised a disproportionate degree of influence. With uncertainties developing in the Atlantic area, some analysts have been encouraged to look speculatively to the Pacific for friends and allies.[42] These geopolitical interests have been augmented by economic factors. The economic growth of Japan and of the Gang of

Four (Singapore, Taiwan, Hong Kong, and Korea), as well as by the emergence of the People's Republic of China, have led some American commentators to emphasize the commonality of economic interests in the area, such as interests in trade, investment, raw materials, and the resources of the Pacific.[43]

While some Americans have been cocking an eye to the Pacific community concept, some Japanese have also been talking and writing about the possibility of a Pacific community. The elements of similarity in U.S. and Japanese thinking on this subject, however, have been quite deceptive. Whereas Americans would find it hard to divorce the security factor altogether from their thinking about a Pacific community, the Japanese would summarily reject any idea of an overt Pacific alliance that had security overtones. The Pacific community concept was Japan's response to the possibility of putting its economic ties with its neighbors on a firmer footing. Through trade, aid, and technological exchange, the country hoped to hold down the sense of hostility and the threat of isolation that it sensed in others.[44]

In one sense, therefore, the two countries have shared a common bond. Neither has been greatly attracted to the other by ties of history and culture. But neither has wished to be isolated from the other, given their international interests. Both have had reason to try to manage any conflict over industrial raw materials in ways that did not disrupt the larger relationship — but a major dispute over raw materials could still develop. Whether such a dispute is likely to arise depends on many variables. One major variable is the nature of the changes that have been occurring in the structure of the world's commodity markets.

2

THE WORLD OIL MARKET IN TRANSITION

With Japan importing practically all its crude oil from foreign sources and the United States importing a third of its requirements from abroad, the two countries have a major stake in the future evolution of the world oil market. At the same time, accounting together for over half the world's consumption of crude oil and oil products outside the communist countries, each also has a strong interest in the policies and practices of the other in such markets.

The world oil market has been rapidly taking on new characteristics whose implications run very deep. In general, the dominance of U.S.-based firms in those markets has been on the decline and other institutions have filled the vacuum. Taken by itself, that trend says very little about the likelihood of conflict or about the opportunities for cooperation between the two countries. A closer look at the process of change is needed in order to detect its implications for the future.

The Rise and Fall of the International Oil Companies

Stability by agreement. From the oil industry's beginnings over a century ago, the U.S. firms that led the industry and the handful of rivals with whom they shared the world's markets were continuously engaged in a search to hold down their risks. The reasons for the emphasis on stability were evident. This has been an industry that has demanded large lumpy commitments from its entrepreneurs — commitments such as those required to develop an oil field or to build a refinery. Once the commitments were made, operation of the productive facility has entailed high fixed costs, so that small variations in price or in output have had a relatively powerful effect on profits. At the same tme, the short-term elasticities of both supply and demand have been very low. When prices have changed, demand and supply have been slow to respond, so that the price could move a considerable distance before it was checked by market forces.

From their earliest days, therefore, the big oil companies looked on unregulated oil markets with a special sense of unease. It was largely this uneasiness that led the two or three leading U.S. firms in 1928 to join their competitors in the Middle East in creating the world oil cartel of 1928. From the viewpoint of the U.S. firms, the operations of their British, Dutch, and French rivals — along with the sporadic sales of the newly established Soviet Union — represented a strong threat to the stability of world markets. Responding to that threat, the leading multinational oil companies put in place a control structure that succeeded in stabilizing the world oil market for over a decade, until the outbreak of World War II put an end to the arrangement.

The experience of those years of relative tranquillity in the oil market suggests some of the difficulties that must be overcome in order to stabilize the market for a commodity such as oil. At that time, the number of sellers in international markets was comparatively small; three or four companies controlled 90 percent of the oil moving in international trade. Yet remarkably elaborate arrangements were required to keep these three or four companies moving in step. One set of arrangements was directed to ensuring that the world's oil production did not exceed the amount that the oil companies thought they could sell at a price satisfactory to them. Another set of arrangements was fashioned to ensure that each of the participants in the market could be relied on to limit its competition, so that the price structure would not be impaired.

As one element in the system of production control, the major international oil companies entered into the so-called red-line agreement, an agreement that created a partnership among them in the Middle East. By itself, the agreement could not have led to the control of production all over the world. To achieve that objective, the participants had to be sure that compatible restraints would be applied to production in other important centers, such as Venezuela and the United States. These links were in fact achieved, but not without considerable effort on the part of the oil majors. The U.S. restraints were put in place during the early 1930s by a system of state-directed proration schemes.[1] The Venezuelan restraints were assured by a system of interlocking ownerships that involved the principal firms participating in the Middle East agreement. The other key agreement of 1928, the "as is" agreement, was designed to provide the necessary assurance against destabilizing competition. This was an agreement in principle among the company heads to freeze their respective shares in each of the markets in which they were selling their products. To be operational, however, the agreement required extensive elaborations market by market, often requiring a specification of shares for each selling enterprise product by product and channel by channel.[2]

Perhaps the most complex structure to be put in place in the 1930s, however, was a pricing mechanism for oil and its products — a mechanism whose role would be understood and acknowledged by all the leading sellers.[3] Because the market price of crude oil was always very much higher than the cost of production for a considerable part of the total supply, the risk of an outbreak of price cutting was usually high. At the same time, it was not easy for any seller immediately to detect a case of price cutting by rivals. The various grades and types of crude oil and their numerous products came from many different sources and were sold in scores of different markets. Accordingly, some very clear and easily administered pricing conventions were required if price rivalry was to be avoided. Such conventions could build the confidence of the various sellers in the predictability of their rivals' behavior and could reduce the risk that different sellers might unintentionally offer their wares at different prices in the same market. Moreover, a price structure of that sort could discourage buyers from playing off sellers against one another and from shopping for bargains, thus adding to the security of the control system.

The exact provisions of the price structure of that period are no longer very important.[4] Like OPEC's efforts of the 1970s and 1980s, the system demanded that its participants have access to some key price for crude oil, a price that none of the participants was in a position to control unilaterally. Such a price was provided in the 1930s by a private publication, *Platt's Oilgram*, which regularly published a figure purporting to represent the price of crude oil available for sale to independent buyers free on board (f.o.b.) U.S. ports in the Gulf of Mexico. From the viewpoint of the sellers, that price had one attractive feature that the OPEC market prices of a later era would not share: the prices of *Platt's Oilgram* were formed in the U.S. market, where supply was under the careful month-to-month scrutiny and control of state proration boards who were empowered to fix production limits.

The establishment of a signal price, however, was only a small first step in the creation of a stable system. Oil could come from several different sources; the challenge was to develop a pricing system that did not inadvertently create price competition in any important market. The principal market for oil from the Gulf ports at the time was the U.S. east coast. Accordingly, the first object of any such system was to ensure that oil coming from other sources, notably Venezuela and nearby Caribbean sources, would not be landed at a lower price in the east coast ports. To achieve that objective, the oil companies that were shipping from the Caribbean area took to quoting an f.o.b. price at their Caribbean shipping points which would land their oil in New York at the same price as oil delivered from the Gulf ports to New York. The Caribbean f.o.b. price having been established, the price in any European market was calculated by beginning with the f.o.b. Caribbean price and adding the appropriate ocean freight to the designated European market. The resulting price, it is important to observe, would be charged in that market for oil from all sources, whether from the Caribbean, the Middle East, or the Dutch East Indies.

These calculations, of course, were based on the assumption that all important sellers in the world would fall in with the prescribed pricing practices. Moreover, the system could work only if sellers used approximately the same freight costs in order to calculate the final price appropriate for given destinations. In the absence of some uniform practice in calculating freight costs, such an outcome would have been impossible, inasmuch as the oil was freighted under a variety of different arrangements. For instance, a considerable part of the oil was carried on tankers owned by the sellers themselves, while the rest was carried on ships under chartering contracts of many different sorts. To provide the necessary guide to freight cost changes, the price quotations generated by the London chartering market proved indispensable.

Systems of this sort must not only be universal: they must also constantly be adapted to the changing conditions of the market. In the case of oil, that fact was evident by the close of World War II, as the major oil companies rapidly expanded their production from the relatively low-cost sources of the Persian Gulf. With production from that area becoming a major source of supply, the practice of charging higher prices in the more easterly markets — higher prices for oil delivered to Syria, for instance, than for oil delivered to Greece — eventually became an unsustainable anomaly, an anomaly that was dangerous for the stability of the market. Bitter protests from the British navy, a major customer in the area, provided the immediate occasion for a change. A few years later, pressures from the U.S. government, which by then was buying large quantities of oil for the European Recovery Program, pushed the oil companies further toward quoting a Persian Gulf price.

The nature of the change that the international oil companies adopted served to highlight one source of their flexibility that would distinguish them sharply from national governments and from their state-owned enterprises. The international oil companies were producers of oil from many different places in the globe. For them, the overriding objective was to maintain a stable global system, not to maximize the advantages of any one area over any other. Accordingly, they were quite capable of contemplating changes in their joint arrangements that tipped the balance of advantage from one area to another, secure in the knowledge that their own operations covered both the advantaged and the disadvantaged areas.

The Persian Gulf price that emerged in the latter 1940s was linked to the prices quoted by *Platt's Oilgram* for Gulf of Mexico oil in such a way as to avoid conflict between supplies from the world's two main sources of oil. Given the production capacity of the Persian Gulf oil fields at the time, the oil companies could define the market area that the Persian Gulf oil would serve. That area being more or less determined, the Persian Gulf price was set to generate a delivered price at the boundary of its market area that was equal to oil delivered to the same boundary from the Gulf of Mexico. In the beginning, when the production of the Persian Gulf area was still relatively small, that boundary fell by common consent in the area of Greece; but as the major oil companies expanded their Middle East production, the boundary moved rapidly westward to Italy, then to Britain — and then, by 1950, to the east coast of the United States.

The appearance of Middle East oil in U.S. markets triggered a series of events that eventually brought an end to the unified system for the control of the world's oil markets. And without such unity, maintaining effective control over world prices became much more difficult.

The events that demonstrated the crucial importance of global unity, however, took some decades to unfold.

With the appearance of Middle East oil in the U.S. market, domestic producers whose facilities were confined to the United States had to confront the fact that the importing firms were obtaining the oil at very low prices, far lower than those of U.S. supplies. The appearance of that oil was threatening the position of U.S. producers in their home markets. At the same time, the influence of the state regulatory agencies over the U.S. market was being undermined. The obvious policy response, which the U.S. developed in the 1950s, was to break the U.S. market away from world markets by imposing import restrictions.

With the imposition of import restrictions in the United States, however, the control of the international oil companies over world markets was weakened. A world in which *Platt's Oilgram* and London charter rates determined prices everywhere was a comparatively safe and sheltered world. Insofar as any political forces could determine the Platt prices, they were the regulatory commissions of the various states of the United States; and those commissions were prepared to hear fully and sympathetically any views that the U.S. oil industry wished to express on the subject. With Persian Gulf prices being quoted independently of prices in the Gulf of Mexico, the international oil companies were more vulnerable to the demands of the governments in oil-exporting countries that those prices should be raised.

Stability by alliance and integration. The stability of the system fashioned by the international companies, however, rested not only on its universal reach but also on the ability of each of the enterprises to forge vertical and horizontal links that diversified its sources of crude oil and its markets. In this respect, too, the international companies differed from the state-owned enterprises that would ultimately dispossess them from some of their activities.

To build up their vertical and horizontal links, companies commonly created consortia and partnerships among themselves at various stages of the business. The red-line agreement had, of course, stimulated that approach among the producers in the Middle East. But many important partnerships were developed outside the area.[5] And the suspension of the red-line agreement after World War II did not end the practice of forging such partnerships. During the 1950s and part of the 1960s, the widespread networks that these links created had the effect of reducing the vulnerability of individual firms to the negotiating pressures of governments. These links gave the companies a capacity to make the needed adjustments in order to deal with short-term shocks in the channels of supply, such as the shut-down of the Suez Canal during the 1956 Israeli-Egyptian war.[6]

The vertical structure of each of the enterprises was also a prominent feature of their organization. Each of the leading international oil companies owned or controlled not only the producing oilfields but also most of the refineries on which their business relied; even the tankers and distribution facilities that they employed were usually tied down under long-term arrangements.[7] Such vertical linkages had numerous advantages, which have been fully described in other sources. Some of these advantages would apply to any industry that shared the characteristics of the oil industry — that is, an industry in which the barriers to entry were high, in which the fixed costs of operation were substantial, and in which the environment was full of uncertainties.[8] In these circumstances, any participant that was not vertically integrated faced risks of variation in the sale of the product that were particularly high, and financial consequences from such variation that were especially costly.

In the case of the crude oil industry, all these conditions strongly applied. But there were special conditions in that industry as well, which made vertical integration particularly attractive for the firms involved.[9] The highest barriers to entry lay at the crude production level, where the difficulties of negotiating with host governments and the high risks of exploration for newcomer firms posed particularly formidable obstacles. The refining business offered barriers as well, but these were easier to overcome inasmuch as most refineries at the time were located in the consuming countries. And the distribution business presented even less formidable entry problems.

The strategic problem for the crude oil producers, therefore — an especially serious problem in times of easy supply — was to maintain a distribution system large enough to keep their wells operating at profitable levels. Stated differently, it was in the interests of the majors to curb independent distributors lest their presence tempt sellers of oil products to maintain their volumes by cutting their prices. Downstream entrants could be curbed if the crude oil prices charged to related subsidiaries and to independent third parties were kept relatively high, so high as to compel the refinery and distribution facilities to operate at a loss. That, in fact, appeared to be the policy of the major oil companies through the 1950s and much of the 1960s. But soon thereafter, despite all the safeguards, their control over prices broke down.

The oligopoly's decline. The kind of world oil market that Japan and the United States are likely to face in the future will obviously be profoundly different in some critical respects from the market they have faced in decades past. A central question will be the role that is to be played by the principal oil-exporting countries. That role could greatly affect the chances of conflict or the opportunities for cooperation between the two countries. Speculation of that sort is bound to begin with OPEC.

Objective opinions on the potential of OPEC are hard to come by: nearly every such view has been colored by the position and interests of the observer.[10] On my reading of the evidence, OPEC has always lacked some of the essential ingredients for an effective control mechanism. Its members have been too numerous, with too many differing perceptions of their collective priorities; composed of national governments, the organization has been barred from altering the benefits flowing to any national area relative to any other; and its reach has been much less than global, excluding notably the United States, the North Sea, and Mexico.

The decline of the control of the majors during the 1960s, therefore, left a vacuum that OPEC could not fill. Some of the reasons for the decline of the international oil companies were fairly evident. One was the extraordinary improvements in international travel and communication, improvements that allowed the oil-exporting countries to train large numbers of officials and technicians in the West or to acquire Western expertise through foreign advisers. With foreign advisers' help, for instance, Libya adopted a law governing oil concessions that was a model of legal sophistication. Under its provisions, Libya tended to favor foreign concessionaires that had no alternative sources of foreign oil, a preference that was to greatly enhance the country's bargaining power during the 1960s.

At least as important a cause of the decline in the power of the international oil companies, however, was the sharp increase in the number of private oil companies engaged in foreign production and sale. As was noted earlier, the number of firms that were producing oil in Africa and the Middle East increased rapidly during the 1950s and 1960s. American independents such as Getty Oil, Occidental Oil, and

Marathon Oil, developed substantial producing stakes in North Africa and the Middle East. This was the period, too, in which a Japanese independent, the Arabian Oil Company, made its entry into the Kuwait neutral zone, and in which Azienda Generale Italiana Petroli (AGIP) obtained a foothold in Iran. Table 2.1 reflects the swift change in the structure of the market during this period.

Table 2.1. Crude oil production, by ownership, 1950–1979 (in percent).[a]

	1950	1957	1966	1970	1979
Seven majors	98.2	89.0	78.2	68.9	23.9
Other international oil companies	1.8	11.0	21.8	22.7	7.4
Producing country oil companies	b	b	b	8.4	68.7
Total	100.0	100.0	100.0	100.0	100.0

a. Excluding crude oil produced in the United States and the communist countries.

b. Negligible.

Sources: Adapted from Brian Levy, "World Oil Marketing in Transition," *International Organization* 36, no. 1 (Winter 1982): 117. Also based on M. A. Adelman, *The World Petroleum Market* (Baltimore: Johns Hopkins University Press, 1972), pp. 80–81; Shell Briefing Service, *The Changing World of Oil Supply*, June 1980, p. 7; and the 1970 and 1979 annual reports of leading oil companies.

One sign of the decline in market control during the 1950s and 1960s was the pronounced reduction in the profit margins of the major oil companies. Part of the squeeze came from the fact that the governments of the oil-exporting countries seized the occasion repeatedly to demand a larger share of the majors' profits in the sale of crude oil.[11] Part came from the independents' offering their oil products in Western Europe and elsewhere at depressed prices. Accordingly, from a level of about 80 cents per barrel in the early 1950s, the majors' net profits per barrel fell to 53 cents in 1960 and 32 cents in 1972.[12] At first, the declining profit margins were more than offset by increases in the volume of sales. But by the latter 1960s, it began to appear that sales increases could not be counted on much longer to offset the declining profit margins. The multinationals were in trouble.

The weakening of the oligopoly could be laid not only to the rising role of the independent oil companies but also to the emergence of another group noted in Table 2.1, the oil companies of the producing countries themselves. Practically all of these enterprises were state-owned. A few located in the more industrialized countries, such as British National Oil Company and Norway's Statoil, were created from scratch as operating companies. But those in the developing countries were usually created and enlarged by successive acts of expropriation, which step by step shoved aside foreign-owned companies that had been operating in the preempted areas. As a rule, the activities taken on by these state-owned enterprises followed a regular pattern. Very early, they assumed the role of bargaining agents for their respective governments and took over management of some of the local distribution and refining activities. Later, some moved into the more demanding activities of exploration, exploitation, and exportation.[13] By the early 1980s, a dozen or more of these firms had to be counted as significant participants in the international oil trade.

The crisis that erupted in the fall of 1973 can be looked on either as a grand coda signaling the end of the era in which the international oil companies controlled the oil market, or as the overture to a new regime not yet defined. Elements of both existed. Even at that late date, the international oil companies still were distributing a very considerable share of oil that moved in international trade. But their control over prices, which had been weakening for a decade or more before the 1973 episode, was unambiguously ended at that time. It would take another five years and another crisis—that generated by the Iranian revolution and Iran's war with Iraq in 1978 and 1979—to establish the fact that the international oil companies no longer controlled a considerable portion of the channels of distribution.

The Transition

The formation of prices. An unambiguous signal that the oil companies had lost control over the international price of oil occurred in the fall of 1973, during the Israeli-Egyptian war, when the open-market price for oil suddenly went soaring from a little under $3 per barrel to about $10.50.[14] Well before that time, the big multinational networks had begun to send signals to independent buyers (so-called third-party buyers) that such buyers could no longer depend on the multinationals as reliable sources of supply. In a pinch, it was clear, the multinationals would serve their own networks first. The high-priced spot oil market that developed in the 1973 crisis, therefore, was typically the result of deals outside the multinational networks, between state-owned oil companies that were beginning to move into international distribution and panicked buyers such as public utilities, chemical companies, and independent refiners.

At this stage, however, most of the oil from OPEC countries continued to move through the channels of the multinationals rather than the spot market. As long as the posted prices of the oil-exporting countries remained unchanged, the cost of that oil to the companies was not affected. In the fall of 1973, however, following the breathtaking rise in spot prices, the OPEC countries decided unilaterally to raise their posted prices, thereby sharply increasing the cost of crude oil to the multinationals.

What followed in the years from 1973 to 1978 was consistent with the picture of a somewhat unruly oligopoly, composed of a dominant member (Saudi Arabia), a dozen followers barely prepared to acknowledge its leadership, and a large outer circle of producers pricing under the shelter of the oligopoly. It was clear at this stage that the majors had lost control of prices, but not at all clear what organizing force had taken its place. By any measure, prices were more variable during these years than in the years before 1973. Part of the movement was due to changes in the official OPEC price; part was due to the fact that some of the oil-exporting countries, casting an eye on prevailing spot prices, refused to be bound by contract prices and contract quantities previously agreed upon with buyers; but part was due to the fact that each of the producing countries felt even more free than in the past to tinker with its royalty rates, its tax rates, and its other terms of sale. At times, the tinkering was intended to increase the country's revenues. At times, too, some of the oligopoly's members appeared to be engaged in trying to increase their share of the market, a tactic especially dangerous for the stability of the oligopoly. These frequent adjustments, which were typically uncoordinated between countries, continually altered the net costs to buyers, as well as the differences in such costs between different classes of buyers.

The periodic meeting of OPEC after 1973 were largely devoted to trying to keep its members from going their separate ways. Up to that time, however, the implacable antagonisms between Saudi Arabia and Iraq, Iraq and Iran, Iran and Saudi Arabia, and Libya and the conservative Arab oil exporters, coupled with the remoteness of Nigeria, Venezuela, and Indonesia, had prevented the development of the common sense of tolerance that effective oligopolies require of their participants. When oil supplies temporarily tightened or when supplies hung heavy over the market, the various sellers typically struck off on their own.[15] There were times when OPEC efforts seemed briefly to reduce the disparate trends, but at other times the efforts failed. We will never know exactly how the OPEC countries would have behaved in that period if OPEC itself had not existed; but their behavior can easily be explained without much reference to the role of OPEC. In any event, the experience of those years emphasized the difficulties of agreeing on either price ceilings or price floors in a market composed of several dozen sellers with widely disparate motivations selling several dozen different grades of oil in several dozen different countries.

By the time of the 1978 crisis, users of oil around the world had grown accustomed to the fact that oil of a given grade offered in any market no longer had a single price. There were bargains to be had for the assiduous shopper and premiums to be paid by the unwary one; there were, in short, strong incentives for any buyer to learn about the market. Figure 2.1 portrays schematically the kind of pattern that was being generated by the market, a pattern that generated a dis-

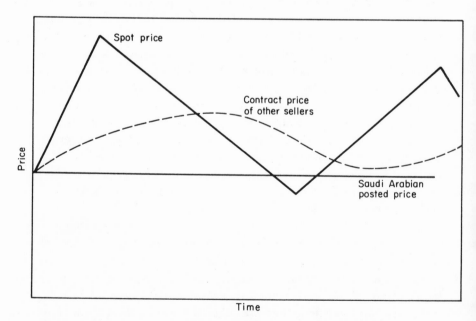

Figure 2.1. Patterns of price behavior in the world crude oil market.

concertingly wide range of prices for a given grade of oil at a given moment from different sources. The events of the 1978 crisis emphasized the fact that the multinational oil companies no longer could guarantee stability either of supply or of price to their customers. Countries such as Japan that were cut off from the supply lines of some of the major oil companies at that time were not losing much in the way of security.

After the 1978 crisis, the continuation of variations in the market price of oil suggested that the pricing problems of OPEC were persisting. In 1981 and again in 1982, after considerable effort, OPEC came to some agreement on posted prices; indeed, the 1982 agreement even included a commitment for the first time to put a lid on production.

Nevertheless, the conditions for maintaining an effective agreement among the sellers were even less propitious than they had been in the 1970s, as some of them confronted compelling pressures to increase their foreign exchange earnings.[16]

The channels of distribution. By the early 1980s, the role of the state-owned companies in the international distribution of oil had grown sufficiently so that one could begin to see some concrete evidence with which to appraise their specific strengths and weaknesses. On the basis of that evidence, it was beginning to appear that such enterprises would have difficulty in maintaining some measure of control over world markets analogous to the earlier control of multinational enterprises.

As Table 2.2 on page 32 indicates, the state-owned enterprises of the oil-exporting countries were selling over 40 percent of the world's oil by the end of the 1970s, leaving a greatly curtailed sphere of operation for the multinationals. Even Saudi Arabia, linked to Western markets by the formidable networks of Aramco's four U.S. partners, was marketing about 30 percent of its oil directly through its state-owned oil company.[17] To be sure, some of the expansion of the state-owned enterprises was not threatening to the core of the multinationals' activities because it entailed nothing more than a takeover of the sales that the multinational firms had been making to independent refiners and distributors. But eventually the state-owned enterprises began cutting into the muscle of the multinationals' operations. Between 1973 and the end of the decade, the multinationals experienced a decline on the order of 7 million barrels daily within their own vertical chains of refineries, petrochemical plants, and gasoline stations.[18]

Nevertheless, the state-owned enterprises had not begun building

Table 2.2. Marketing channels of internationally traded oil for the period 1950–1979 (in percent).

	1950	1957	1966	1973	1976	1979
Marketing by international oil companies:						
Interaffiliate transfers	92.8	82.4	80.0	69.6	59.1	46.6
Third-party sales	7.2	17.6	20.0	22.5	16.3	11.2
Direct marketing by producer countries	a	a	a	7.9	24.6	42.2
Total	100.0	100.0	100.0	100.0	100.0	100.0

a. Negligible.

Sources: Brian Levy, "World Oil Marketing in Transition," *International Organization* 36, no. 1 (Winter 1982): 121; *Petroleum Intelligence Weekly* 19, no. 8 (February 25, 1980): 4.

rival chains of their own in international markets. Instead, they were relying on a variety of independent buyers to absorb their oil. Now and then, one of the established international oil firms entered into an open-market deal with a state-owned enterprise; by 1980 the majors were buying over 10 percent of their own crude oil on the open market. More commonly, the buyers were firms engaged in refining and distributing oil in their own national markets, which formerly had acquired their crude oil from the large international firms. In some cases, the national firms that were importing oil proved to be state-owned, such as Petrobras in Brazil or Hispanoil in Spain. Indeed, some of the state-owned sellers of oil, such as those in Venezuela, Nigeria, and Saudi Arabia, pursued an explicit policy of favoring state-owned buyers.[19] At one point, Saudi Arabia conditioned its sale of oil to Denmark with the provision that Denmark create a state-owned distribution company.[20] And in 1982 the Saudi Arabian state-owned exporter announced that it would sell only to buyers officially designated by the importing countries.[21]

Some of the direct sales by state-owned enterprises were made on the spot market as isolated tanker shipments; all told, that kind of sale amounted to one or two million barrels daily. Most sales were made under contracts that stipulated some stated quantity to be shipped over a period of several months. These longer-run commitments sometimes were arranged as part of an even larger framework in which governments undertook to supply and acquire very large quantities of oil. In

1978, for instance, the Japanese government negotiated with Mexico just such a framework, which entailed the financing of petrochemical plants, rail lines, and port facilities, as well as large-scale loans to Mexican borrowers; in return, the Japanese could look forward to sales over the long term that might eventually reach 300,000 barrels per day.[22] At about the same time, Mexico undertook similar broad-ranging deals with France, Brazil, and several other countries.

Arrangements of this sort, however, often failed to provide anything like the degree of security that buyers or sellers were seeking. In 1980, for example, in spite of the framework accord, Mexico cut back sharply on shipments to Japan. And when France refused to accept a price increase for Mexican oil late in 1981, Mexico threatened to cut off France's participation in subway, steel, and automobile projects in Mexico.[23]

The firm-to-firm contracts issued by state-owned enterprises, as it turned out, also proved fragile. As noted earlier, when prices stiffened, sellers repeatedly refused to perform pursuant to such contracts.[24] Before 1973, in the era when multinational oil companies controlled the market, buyers could respond to such a contingency by trying to develop and control their own upstream supplies. But by 1980 that possibility rarely existed, except perhaps in the United States.

For any enterprise whose fortunes depended on a steady supply of oil, therefore, the markets of the early 1980s were seen as high-risk markets. Various efforts were afoot to try to reduce those risks. For instance, in the early 1980s public markets were established in New York and London to provide a market for dealing in oil futures; a market of that sort, it was hoped, might provide a means of buffering buyers and sellers against uncertainty. But early reports on the functioning of that market were not very encouraging.[25] And experiences with other such markets, such as the London Metals Exchange markets in copper, suggested that these facilities would do little to contribute to market stability and might even have a contrary effect by attracting destabilizing speculation.

Nor did it seem likely that the inventory policies of the intermediary firms in the oil business would provide a new source of stability. At times, such firms drew on their inventories to supply a tight market; but at other times, they seemed to be building up their inventories for speculative profits.[26] Some ameliorating factors, to be sure, were slightly blunting the threat of price instability. Official stockpiles had

Table 2.3. Capital and exploration expenditures on crude oil and natural gas by the w petroleum industry, 1964–1980.[a]

	1964–1968		1969–1973		1974–1978		1979–198	
	Amount (in millions of dollars)	Percent	Amount (in millions of dollars)	Percent	Amount (in millions of dollars)	Percent	Amount (in millions of dollars)	Pe⟩
United States	19,425	67.5	24,850	58.8	65,595	53.2	56,500	5
Other Western Hemisphere countries	4,560	15.9	7,200	17.0	17,830	14.5	18,300	I
Western Europe	925	3.2	3,000	7.1	21,425	17.4	17,700	I
Middle East	1,375	4.8	2,400	5.7	6,825	5.5	4,150	
Other	2,485	8.6	4,800	11.4	11,600	9.4	9,150	
Total	28,770	100.0	42,250	100.0	123,275	100.0	105,800	1C

a. Excludes communist areas.
Source: Chase Manhattan Bank, Energy Economics Division, "Capital Investments o World Petroleum Industry," annual brochure, all issues 1964 to 1980.

grown somewhat, especially among the OECD countries. But by and large, the sense of insecurity among users was high.

One trend from which users could take some comfort was the shift in the geographical location of the capital and exploration expenditures being made by the world's oil industry in the production of crude oil and gas. As Table 2.3 shows, that pattern shifted after the 1973 crisis. The long-term trend in the relative decline of the United States was checked. Western Europe's position, based mainly on North Sea activity, rose considerably. The area that lost substantially in relative position was the Middle East, of course. To be sure, the geographical shift in development expenditures represented no guarantee that production would shift to the same degree. But from the users' viewpoint, the shift offered the prospect of some increased measure of security in the medium term.

Besides, by the early 1980s there were already some signs that the added efforts of producers to bring in oil from safe areas was beginning to have some considerable effects on the patterns of current production. In 1973 the thirteen OPEC countries had accounted for about 67 percent of the world's crude oil production outside the communist countries. By 1981, however, their contribution had dropped to 50 percent, lower than it had been since the early 1960s. And the prospective figure for 1982, assuming they adhered to their agreed production ceiling, would decline further to about 40 percent. The margins of influence and margins of safety for the OPEC countries, although still very large, were considerably reduced.

From the viewpoint of some of the oil-exporting countries, the resurgence of development activities in various "safe" areas of the world suggested that their own postions might prove more precarious in the course of time. Accordingly, they began to explore measures to protect such positions. In their efforts to reduce their reliance on the multinationals, practically all major oil-exporting countries had very early developed plans for building downstream facilities (oil refineries and petrochemical plants) on their own home territory, and for assembling their own tanker fleets.[27] That strategy, however, was more relevant for periods of shortage than for periods of surplus. In shortage, it freed the oil exporters from any reliance on the refining and distributing facilities of the multinationals and placed the exporters in a position of denying the multinationals any share of the extraordinary profits available in such periods. In surplus, however, the oil exporters still had to face the risk that their products might be displaced in importing countries, either by official restrictions on imports or by the competitive offerings of others.

Worries of this sort, when coupled with the needs of the oil exporters for help in acquiring the requisite technology and management to run their enterprises, probably explain why the oil-exporting countries were often willing to bring foreign partners ino the new refineries and petrochemical complexes that they were setting up on their home soil.[28] Links between state-owned enterprises and foreign oil companies appeared throughout the world, in many different forms: sometimes in joint ventures, sometimes in long-term service contracts, sometimes in more ambiguous relationships. In some instances the new partnerships were with the very multinationals that they had dispossessed from crude oil operations. Exxon, for instance, developed new links with Venezuela; Gulf Oil and British Petroleum retained ties with Kuwait; and Mobil moved into various downstream operations with Saudi Arabia.

The oil exporters were still faced, however, with the need to obtain more secure assurances of their ability, in the event of surplus, to protect their competitive positions in foreign markets. Neither OPEC's muscle nor long-term contractual arrangements nor the creation of processing facilities on their own soil seemed likely to provide the requisite assurances. Another kind of strategy still remained to each of the state-owned enterprises, one that the multinational enterprises themselves had favored in years gone by. This was for each state-owned enterprise to acquire its own refineries and distribution facilities in the markets of the importing countries.

The beginnings of such a strategy had already been visible before the revolution that toppled the shah in Iran, when the National Iranian Oil Company (NIOC) began to acquire distribution facilities abroad; in joint ventures with private firms or with other state-owned enterprises NIOC acquired downstream facilities in India, South Africa, and Senegal. Meanwhile, the state-owned enterprise of Abu Dhabi made similar arrangements in Pakistan, as did Mexico's Petroleos Mexicanos in Spain. The tendency picked up momentum in the 1980s, as the Kuwait Petroleum Company acquired interests in various refining and engineering facilities in the United States.[29]

It was uncertain, however, whether arrangements of that sort would go very far. In some respects, state-owned enterprises were more limited in their choice of strategies than private multinational enterprises. When the strategy entailed investment in foreign countries, state-owned enterprises had to be responsive to the commands of their governments. Some governments would find it hard to authorize downstream investment by the state-owned enterprises in oil-importing countries; the Mexican and Venezuelan governments, for instance, would have great difficulty in authorizing such investments in the U.S. market. Moreover, despite the fact that state-owned British Petroleum, Elf-Aquitaine, and AGIP managed to make heavy investments in foreign markets, it was not at all clear that downstream investments on a significant scale by state-owned oil companies from the OPEC countries would share the same kind of welcome.

The Prospects

Despite the efforts of buyers and sellers to reintroduce some measure of stability in the market, therefore, the likelihood of continued instability is fairly high. On the supply side, variations in price have done little to evoke stabilizing reactions. In the short run, price increases have not expanded supply nor have price declines reduced it; the marginal costs of oil and oil products to major suppliers are so low relative to the market price as to be irrelevant to price determinations. On the demand side, price elasticities in the short run have also been very low.

Nor is the market likely to develop stability by agreement among the participants. Although OPEC is attempting valiantly to fill the breach, its success seems unlikely. The number of sellers in the market appears too large, their interests too disparate. Each state-owned enterprise is in some degree a creature of its government; many governments are unwilling to tie themselves to the elaborate long-term agreements that would be needed to bring stability to the market; and even if they were, it seems altogether unlikely that the participants could develop the level of mutual trust required of the participants in a successful oligopoly.

Gaining stability through long-term bilateral agreements, as some buying and selling countries hope to do, seems equally chimerical. Such agreements have proved fragile under pressure, whether from the pressure of spot prices or from the pressure of political frictions.

Japan and the United States, therefore, seem to be confronting international oil markets that differ in two key respects from the markets of earlier decades. First, the threat of price instability appears much greater than in the past. Second, the degree of concentration among the sellers is lower and their policies more loosely coordinated. In later chapters, these changes will be discussed in terms of the reactions of the United States and Japan, in an effort to determine their implications. For the present, however, we turn to the hard minerals to learn whether analogous developments have occurred in those markets.

3

CHANGING
WORLD MARKETS
IN MINERALS
AND METALS

As any expert in the metals markets will insist, no two such markets are quite alike. In concentrating on aluminum, copper, and steel, therefore, there is some risk that we will have narrowed the focus of the inquiry too much, overlooking the possibilities of some major problems in other metals or their related ores. The three metals, however, do offer considerable coverage. In the case of the United States, the imports of raw materials or raw material equivalents accounted for by the three products represent about 70 percent of all nonfuel mineral imports. In the case of Japan, they represent 80 percent of such imports. And the similarities that find their way through the complex mosaic presented by each of the three industries suggest the existence of strong general tendencies that apply even more widely. In all these cases, the possibility of sellers' maintaining effective control over the supply of the minerals appears to have declined, while the prospects for instability in the prices of the minerals appear to have increased.

The Industries' Characteristics

Some of the characteristics that give these industries a central position in the lives of industrialized countries are obvious. Each industry produces a metal that contributes heavily to advanced industrial activities and to military capabilities. In addition, Japan and the United States rely heavily on imports for their needed supplies in the three

Table 3.1. Structure of three industries, late 1970s.[a]

Industry	Degree of concentration: percent of world capacity accounted for by		Ownership patterns: percent of world mining capacity in market economies owned by		Prevalence of vertical integration in 8 largest firms: number of firms with substantial operations at all major stages
	4 largest firms	8 largest firms	Private firms	State-owned firms	
Aluminum					
Bauxite	48.6	68.6	78	22	6
Alumina	51.5	71.7	88	12	
Aluminum	43.3	61.9	83	17	
Iron and steel					
Iron ore	37.3	62.1	80	20	1
Steel	21.2	33.4	b	b	
Copper					
Copper mining	37.6	55.4	59	41	5
Copper smelting	34.0	53.3	b	b	
Copper refining	27.4	46.4	b	b	

a. Omits communist countries.

b. Not available.

Source: Adapted from UNIDO, *Mineral Processing in Developing Countries* (New York, 1980).

industries, a dependency that will not diminish in the future (see Appendix, Table 2).

There are other reasons why a review of the three metals and their related ores provides a useful focus. Like most metals, all three demand highly capital-intensive facilities and very large-scale operations in their production. At the same time, however, the three industries are somewhat unlike each other in industrial structure (see Table 3.1). From that point of view, they represent a diverse set of cases.

In bauxite and alumina, six huge firms dominate the world markets — three from the United States, two from Europe, and one from Canada. Each of the six is linked to its sources of bauxite and alumina by ties of ownership, commonly through joint ventures. As a result, about three-quarters of the bauxite and alumina that move in international channels represent transactions between affiliates, and no open competitive market for these materials has yet developed.[1]

The iron ore industry offers a second pattern. In this case, vertical integration within a single country is very common; vertical integration across international borders is much less so. Accordingly, of the iron ore that moves in international trade, only 20 percent consists of captive shipments.[2] But because the physical and chemical composition of iron ore is quite diverse, iron ore has not yet developed a broad public market.

The copper industry of the world presents a somewhat different story. It is less highly concentrated in ownership than the aluminum industry, and displays less vertical integration between the mines and the mills. About two-fifths of the mining output is in the hands of state-owned enterprises, whose links to the copper smelters and fabricators in importing countries are tenuous. Not surprisingly, therefore, sales of copper ore and concentrates between independent parties are relatively common, much more so than in bauxite and alumina. What is more, copper materials have a relatively high value by weight, and can move considerable distances in international trade. As a result, these materials can be bought on a world market in which real price competition exists. The price of copper, quoted on the London Metals Exchange (LME), is of major importance to sellers of copper ore and concentrates.

With three such diverse industries, it would not have been surprising to find that the industries had developed in quite different directions. As it turns out, however, the direction of change of the three industries has been quite similar, creating a fairly solid basis for generalization.

The Emergence of International Industries

As in oil, U.S. firms figured prominently in the creation of international industries in the various metals. Aluminum, copper, and iron ore industries were developed on the basis of rich national endowments of raw materials, including a combination of cheap energy and cheap ore. In 1920 the United States was producing 62 percent of the world's copper, 48 percent of its aluminum, and 60 percent of its steel, drawing heavily on domestic raw materials.

Outside the United States, the firms participating in these industries commonly held the risks of international competition in check by developing cartel agreements. By the 1920s these international cartels characteristically had developed overt or clandestine links with the major U.S. firms. Some of these cartel arrangements were effective for a while; some were more fragile. Whether the restrictive arrangements would succeed depended to a considerable extent on the structure of the industry.

Aluminum represented one of the more successful restrictive arrangements. The basis for that success, as nearly as can be discerned, was the clear dominance of one or two major firms in the industry and the limited number of junior participants.[3] The world leader of the industry was the firm that would later acquire the name of Aluminum Company of America, headquartered in the United States; eventually, Alcoa would be obliged to spin off its Canadian subsidiary as a separate entity. In Europe, France's Pechiney dominated the industry. To be sure, even before World War II, aluminum producers were to be found in other countries, including Germany and Switzerland; but these were small and high-cost in relation to the leaders.

Unlike other metals such as copper and nickel, the leaders in aluminum did not rely heavily on their access to cheap ore as a basis for maintaining their leadership. Because bauxite represented only about 10 percent of the value of the aluminum metal,[4] supplies of rich ore were not critically important. Much more important was access to large quantities of cheap power, the mastery of a complex technology, and the ability to invest in large capital-intensive facilities. Nevertheless, when major deposits of rich ore were found in various Caribbean areas in the early part of the century, the North American fabricators strengthened their leadership positions in the industry by developing these sources.

These advantages, when taken together, represented formidable barriers that helped bolster the security of the industry leaders. Yet even in this instance, members of the industry felt the need to develop explicit cartel agreements among them, limiting production and fixing prices. The first such agreement was created in 1896, and the agreements were renewed several times in the next thirty-five years.[5]

The iron and steel industry, like the aluminum industry, succeeded in developing some effective measures to control international competition. But in the case of iron and steel, the barriers that stifled competition and helped make its cartel a success were of rather a different kind.

As with aluminum, the U.S. iron and steel industry began with rich endowments of raw materials, including the iron ore of the Mesabi range and coal from accessible deposits in the Appalachian area and the midwest. But the early start of the Europeans in this industry during the nineteenth century kept the American firms inward-looking and insular. These firms had no difficulty falling in with the elaborate cartel mechanism that the Europeans constructed and maintained through the early decades of the twentieth century.[6] The insular quality that was fostered in the U.S. steel industry during these formative years, in fact, would persist for decades in the cultures of its leading firms, making them among the most protectionist of the various industry groups.[7] Some slight willingness on the part of the steel firms to move out beyond their respective national environments in a search for iron ore would eventually appear — but not until after World War II, when technological improvements in transportation and communication had begun to shrink the distances between nations.

In the copper industry, the difficulties of maintaining an effective cartel for very long manifested themselves quite early. As in aluminum and steel, a small number of U.S. firms at first seemed to dominate the industry. But the barriers to the entry of newcomers in this instance were not very high. Copper smelters and refineries were not notably difficult in technological terms or demanding in capital terms. Copper ore bodies were to be found in a number of locations. Eventually some of the mines came under the control of outsiders. By 1927 the mines of Zambia (then Northern Rhodesia) were being developed by independent British and American interests, and independent smelters and refiners were appearing in Europe and North America. Although a succession of international cartels was created in copper between the two world wars, the diffusion of sources of supply and processing facilities was enough to undermine the structure.[8]

The Decline of the Multinational Enterprises

Preparing the way. World War II marked a critical breaking point in the continuity of the metals and minerals industries, just as it did in the oil industry. The elaborate cartel arrangements that had persistently appeared and reappeared in the three metals seemed almost totally suppressed, victims partly of the the war's disruptions and partly of some of the critical antitrust suits initiated by the United States.

The postwar period brought a surge of new growth in the various metal industries. In the first expansive phase of this postwar sequence, the established aluminum and copper firms were especially active and almost seemed to be regaining some of their prewar control. Alcoa, still the world's leader, put alumina plants in Jamaica and other Caribbean locations. Other leading aluminum firms established mining operations, either alone or in consortia, not only in the Caribbean but also in Australia, Greece, Guinea, and Sierra Leone. In copper, Anaconda greatly expanded its Chilean operations, while Asarco and others joined in expanding Peru's copper mines.

At this stage even the leading steel firms of Europe and the United States, normally nation-bound and protectionist, developed some mining facilities on foreign soil. To be sure, the overseas ventures of the steel firms seemed relatively conservative at the time, in terms of the political risks they entailed. For the U.S. firms, the largest developments were in nearby Canada, where most of the major American steel producers made direct investments in mining properties. In addition, there were new developments in Liberia; there Bethlehem Steel joined in a partnership with the Liberian government and the leading Swedish enterprise in iron ore mining, while Republic Steel joined the Liberian government in another venture. German and Luxembourgian firms developed mining and pelletizing interests in Brazil. In Venezuela, too, both U.S. Steel and Bethlehem Steel developed extensive mining facilities; and for a time it appeared that U.S. Steel might also establish itself in a joint venture in Brazil.[9]

In the brief flurry of postwar expansion, the leading aluminum and copper firms also pushed downstream into the fabricating end of the business. The aluminum companies were bolder in their strategies than the copper companies, probably reflecting their greater sense of security. Alcan and Alcoa substantially expanded their direct investments in fabricating companies. The copper refiners, following a different approach to integration, sought to tie the fabricators to them by offering to buffer the fabricators against some of the fluctuations in the world price for refined copper. The refiners offered to sell at so-called producers' prices, rather than at the prices quoted on the London Metals Exchange; producers' prices, it was anticipated, would be more stable than the LME price, rising less rapidly in periods of shortage and falling less rapidly in glut.

The flurry of strength on the part of the multinational mining firms, however, proved quite short-lived. While the multinational enterprises were expanding their foreign positions and increasing their vertical links, the number of mining and refining firms was steadily increasing, as was the number of countries from which they originated. In copper, the big three U.S.-based firms, which had accounted for 28 percent of the world's copper refining capacity in 1956, held only 14 percent of the world's refining capacity in 1975; in the same period, the capacity of the mines under their control slipped from 36 percent to 23 percent of the world total. In aluminum, the six largest producers found their share of smelter capacity in the noncommunist world slipping from 85 percent in 1956 to 58 percent in 1975.[10] The increase in numbers and diversity would eventually make any system of collective control increasingly difficult to maintain.

But the increase in the number of mining firms was not the only factor that weakened their position. After World War II, the governments of various countries in which mining properties were located began to see alternatives to the multinational enterprise. In the 1960s, many governments were in a position to acquire needed funds from public lending institutions such as the World Bank; and in the 1970s, even the private Eurodollar markets were ready to finance such ventures. During this period, too, the greatly improved facilities for international communication and travel allowed governments in the developing countries more readily to train their engineers abroad or to bring in foreign experts as needed. By the early 1970s, for instance, over 20 percent of the doctoral degrees conferred by U.S. universities in the science and engineering fields were going to foreign students, and in Europe nearly 50 percent of the university students in science and engineering were of foreign origin.[11] Although a considerable proportion of the foreigners came from industrialized countries, third-world countries were heavily represented.

With technical skills beginning to spread and with capital more readily available, the only thing that the exporting countries still had to acquire in order to be free of the foreign enterprises was an ability to market the ore. Here, too, time and technology seemed on the side of the exporters. During the 1950s and 1960s the world's aluminum, copper, and steel industries, main users of the metallic ores, were all exhibiting signs of deconcentration; new producing firms and new producing countries were rapidly appearing. Japan was, of course, the largest new buyer of these metal ores to appear in that period. Unlike the Americans and the Europeans, however, the Japanese did not divert much capital or managerial attention to the actual operation of mining properties on foreign soil. Instead, by various means, Japanese buyers encouraged others to finance and operate the mines. Japanese needs, therefore, opened up vast opportunities for new independent sellers: in iron ore, for firms operating in Australia, India, and Venezuela; in copper, for firms in Australia, Bougainville, Zambia, Peru, and Chile; in bauxite, for firms in Australia; and so on.

The sense of independence of the exporters of metallic ores was increased in some cases during the 1950s and 1960s by another new factor — namely, the development of home industries that could process the ores into metal. Brazil and India developed large steel industries, and practically all copper ore exporters developed their own copper smelters. Aluminum smelters were a little slower to appear outside the mature industrialized countries in the ore-exporting countries; but these, too, eventually joined the new trend. A few countries with bauxite ore secured such smelters in the 1970s, and by the 1980s smelters were beginning to appear in oil-producing countries with ample supplies of flare gas.

The nationalization wave. With the appearance of Japan and others in foreign markets as alternative buyers for metallic ores and with the growth of domestic ore-using industries in the ore-exporting countries, it was only a matter of time before some of the countries whose mining facilities were under the control of foreign enterprises would begin to consider how to take control of the facilities.

In copper, the problem of market access could still give some pause to the producing countries, inasmuch as the fabricators in the copper-using countries were to a considerable extent under the control of the big copper companies of the United States and Europe. Nevertheless, there were times when the marketing problem seemed to lift. Accordingly, when striking miners made copper temporarily short in the latter 1960s, Zaire, Chile, and Zambia were emboldened to plunge into the nationalization of their foreign-owned mines. (see Table 3.2 on pages 46 and 47). When raw materials prices surged upward during 1970 and 1971, the price movement brought on another wave of mining nationalizations. That wave was followed by more cases in 1973 and 1974, an echo of the nationalizations that were occurring at that time in the oil industry.

Once the big copper companies lost control of their mines, their position in the industry was undermined. Recall that during the 1950s and 1960s the copper refiners of the United States and elsewhere had extended their vertical links in various ways: they had expanded their mining operations in foreign countries and they had linked themselves to copper fabricators and other copper users by undertaking to supply

Table 3.2. Major nationalizations in bauxite, iron ore, and copper ore enterprises, 1965–1982.

Country	Date	Companies affected	Share nationalized (in percent)
Bauxite			
Ghana	1972	British Aluminium (U.K.)	55
		Reynolds (U.S.)	55
		Union Carbide (U.S.)	55
Guinea	1972–73	Olin-Mathieson (U.S.)	49
		British Aluminium (U.K./U.S.)	49
		Schweizerische Aluminium AG (W. Germany)	49
		Pechiney-Ugine-Kuhlmann (France)	49
Guyana	1970	Alcan (Canada)	100
	1974	Reynolds (U.S.)	100
	1976	Alcoa (U.S.)	100
Jamaica	1974	Alcoa (U.S.)	6
		Alcan (Canada)	7
		Kaiser (U.S.)	51
		Reynolds (U.S.)	51
Surinam	1974	Reynolds (U.S.)	a
Iron Ore			
Chile	1971	Bethlehem (U.S.)	100
		Armco (U.S.)	100
Gabon	1974	Bethlehem (U.S.)	a
Mauritania	1974	Usinor and others (France) Bureau de Recherches Géologiques et Minières (France)	a
		British Steel	a
		Finsider (Italy)	a
		Thyssen (Germany)	a
Peru	1975	Cyprus Mines Corp. (U.S.)	100
		Utah International (U.S.)	100
Venezuela	1974	United States Steel (U.S.)	100
	1974	Bethlehem Steel (U.S.)	100

Table 3.2 continued.

Country	Date	Companies affected	Share nationalized (in percent)
Copper			
Chile	1967	Kennecott (U.S.)	51
	1967	Anaconda (U.S.)	25
	1967	Cerro de Pasco (U.S.)	30
	1969	Anaconda (U.S.)	51
	1971	Anaconda (U.S.)	51
	1971	Kennecott (U.S.)	100
	1971	Cerro de Pasco (U.S.)	100
Mexico	1971	Anaconda (U.S.)	51
Panama	1975	Canadian Javelin (Canada)	100
Peru	1970	Anaconda (U.S.)	100
	1972	Marcona (U.S.)	100
	1974	Cerro de Pasco (U.S.)	100
Zaire	1966	Union Minière (Belgium)	a
Zambia	1970	Anglo-American (S. Africa)	a
	1970	Amax (U.S)	51
	1973	Amax (U.S.)	49
	1973	Anglo-American (S. Africa)	49
Uganda	1975	Commonwealth Development (U.K./Canada)	90

a. Not available.

Sources: Various documents of the United Nations Secretariat, especially the Centre on Transnational Corporations; compilations by Stephen Kobrin, New York University; S. D. Krasner, *Defending the National Interest* (Princeton, N.J.: Princeton University Press, 1978), p. 44.

them with the metal at producers' prices. Sometimes these prices were lower than the contemporary price on the London Metals Exchange, at other times higher. The refiners' loss of control over their own foreign mines in the 1960s and 1970s weakened their ability to provide copper at stable prices, and a precipitate rise in the costs of power and labor in the 1970s finished the system off. Because of the weak structure of the copper oligopoly and the relatively high price elasticity of demand for copper, the refiners found themselves unable to pass the whole increase in costs on to consumers. As a result, the profitability of the refining operation fell sharply.[12] Under the squeeze, U.S. refiners in 1977 finally abandoned the practice of offering producers' prices for the copper metal, insisting that henceforth they would charge the open-market LME price. That action cut back the extensive quasi-integration that had been practiced by the industry.

A somewhat similar process, less pervasive in extent and effect, occurred in iron ore, as Chile, Peru, and Venezuela divested U.S. firms of their mining properties. In this case, however, the results were more complex. The principal reaction of the U.S. firms was to turn back to safer — albeit higher-cost — sources of ore in the United States and Canada, while retaining a vertical structure. European and Japanese firms, meanwhile, seemed less deterred by the nationalizations, developing new links in several countries. As in the past, the Japanese continued to avoid actually operating foreign mines, limiting their participation instead to long-term purchase contracts and to a modest financing role.[13] All told, as U.S. firms retreated and Japanese firms came to represent a larger share of the world steel industry, there was an overall decline in the vertical integration of the industry.

In bauxite and alumina a slight weakening in vertical structure also occurred, largely as a result of the various nationalizations of Guyana, Guinea, and Jamaica. In this case, the aluminum smelters were relatively few in number, and hence the marketing problem persisted for a longer time as a serious hurdle to nationalization. The importance of that factor as a deterrent to nationalization was illustrated by Guyana's exceptionally early nationalization of some of its bauxite mines. Guyana felt itself in a position to move early because about half of Guyana's output was not dependent on the aluminum smelters as a market. That half consisted of calcine bauxite, which was marketed to hundreds of brick refractories that used the material in the fabrication of heat-resistant brick.

The Drive for Stability

The growing dispersion among the producers of metal ores and the shrinkage in the vertical links between buyers and sellers of the ores produced a major restructuring of the three industries. Figure 3.1 reflects some of these changes. The indexes in Figure 3.1 are so-called Herfindahl indexes, whose exact values and definitions are presented in Table 3 of the appendix. Briefly, these indexes are a standard measure of industry concentration, based on the global output or global ca-

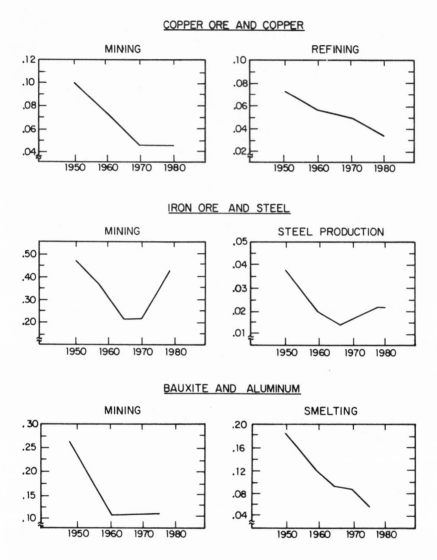

Figure 3.1. Herfindahl indexes of concentration of world production in three industries, 1950–1980.

pacity of the individual firms producing in the indicated industry; when concentration in the industry declines, the index falls. As the figure shows, concentration declined sharply in the aluminum and copper industries throughout the period, the result of the appearance of new comers and the weakening of the old leaders. In iron ore and steel, the pattern was more complex. At first, the relative decline of the established leaders also produced a fall in the concentration of the industry, so that ore users like Japan had an increased range of choices in their buying. Eventually, however, the rapid growth of Australia's major iron ore mines reversed the deconcentration trend in mining, while the growth of Japan's leading steel firms reversed the deconcentration trend in steel production. Thereafter, Japan and Australia found themselves in a position of mutual dependence, with the bargaining strength distributed between them.

In some circumstances, changes in structure of the sort experienced in these industries might have been conducive to more price stability rather than less, as increased numbers of buyers and sellers participated in the formation of prices. In the case of these three industries, however, the changes proved threatening to price stability. Although the organization of the aluminum, steel, and copper industries was greatly changed, their technological characteristics were not. They remained highly capital-intensive industries, with high fixed costs and low variable costs, whose enterprises therefore were unusually vulnerable to small variations in output levels. A decline in the degree of vertical integration of these industries increased the exposure of buying and selling firms to such variations. At the same time, although the producers and users of these various ores were no longer small enough in number to allow for effective stabilization schemes, neither were they yet so numerous as to offer the promise of an efficient open market. From time to time, outbreaks of rivalrous buying and selling by leading firms produced spasms of instability in the various markets for ores and metals.

Fixing prices. By the latter 1960s, some of the consequences of the new uncertainties could be seen in the markets for most metal and minerals. Again, the results were particularly striking in the case of copper. During the 1950's, while remnants of the old copper oligopoly were still in evidence, the leading firms were repeatedly engaged if efforts to maintain stability. From time to time, the press reported meetings between the major European producers and "Chilean authorities" to discuss strategies for stabilizing prices and controlling production.[14] (The "Chilean authorities," it was widely assumed, were stand-ins for the American copper companies operating in that country, whose participation was needed for any effective system of control.)

The wave of nationalizations by Chile, Zaire, Zambia, and Peru in the latter 1960s vastly expanded the position of state-owned enterprises in world production, pushing their share of world mine capacity from 10 percent to over 40 percent. In 1967, as prices fluctuated wildly, the four governments formed the Conseil Intergouvernmental des Pays Exportateurs de Cuivre (CIPEC), which turned promptly to the question of restoring stability to the copper market. But in the years that followed, the special difficulties of state-owned enterprises in agreeing upon a scheme of market control were repeatedly illustrated.

These enterprises found it particularly difficult, for instance, to adjust their production to periods of reduced demand. Cutting back output meant less use of labor, and as a rule the idea of reducing employment in such periods was unacceptable. Accordingly, state-owned enterprises were known to continue producing in periods of falling demand and to continue selling on world markets, with especially destructive effects on price.[15]

In aluminum, the efforts of the producers to keep the market under control were unremitting throughout the postwar period. Even before the bauxite-exporting countries became a factor in the industry, the European producers cooperated closely in keeping the market stable.[16] Organizations such as the European Producers' Aluminium Association and the International Primary Aluminium Association and the International Primary Aluminium Institute took active measures to avoid the construction of excess smelting capacity and to hold surplus metal off the market. The consortium structure to which aluminum producers so commonly resorted in the development of bauxite mines and alumina plants made such efforts a little easier. But the industry was not immune from the effects of its deconcentrating tendencies, and by the early 1970s there was widespread concern over weakening prices.[17]

In 1974 a number of state-owned enterprises, which had recently entered the industry, joined with other bauxite-producing areas in the creation of an eleven-member International Bauxite Association (IBA). That association, however, was no more successful in controlling the price of bauxite than was CIPEC in copper. But the reasons for the lack of success in bauxite were different. In the case of bauxite, governments could not overlook the fact that most of the product still moved in tight vertical channels from mines to related alumina plants to related aluminum smelters. In view of the highly concentrated structure in the smelter stage of the industry, it would have been utterly reckless for governments in the bauxite-exporting countries to cut themselves off from their established channels. Accordingly, four years of negotiation in IBA produced nothing more than an agreement among its members not to agree on the pricing of bauxite.[18] As far as the industry was concerned, such stability as existed would still depend mainly on how long the smelters could retain control over the market.

In iron ore, the problems of instability that accompanied the entry of state-owned enterprises into the market were not apparent for some time. In this instance, state-owned enterprises increased their share of the world's output from trivial quantities in 1950 to 26 percent of output in 1978. By the latter date, Japan and the European countries were receiving over one-third of their imported ore from state-owned mines, and the United States was receiving over one-quarter of its imported ore from such sources. In this case, however, the principal state-owned mining enterprises were strong sellers; located mainly in Brazil, Venezuela, India, and South Africa, they were not under the same compulsions as the copper enterprises to sell in declining markets.

Nevertheless, even in the case of iron ore, sellers exhibited various signs of concern over the stability of the market. The highly concentrated structure of demand represented one kind of threat; in 1975, for instance, the world's four largest importing entities accounted for 69 percent of the international ore trade.[19] The privately owned mines of Australia, Canada, and the United States — some vertically integrated to the steel mills, others selling to the mills under long-term arrangements — represented another threat. Not surprisingly, therefore, the producing governments in 1975 huddled together in a structure that paralleled the copper producers, creating the Association of Iron Ore Exporters. But Australia's unwillingness to consider joint cartel action prevented any serious efforts in that direction, and by the early 1980s there was no evidence that the organization was capable of performing a stabilizing role.[20]

Restoring captive markets. It was evident by the early 1980s that the principal parties in the mining and metals industries were still greatly concerned with the threat of instability in their respective markets.

Moreover, there was a strong presumption, supported by recent history, that stability could not be restored by horizontal agreements among producers; the cartel approach could not provide anything like the market power that the parties desired. The existence of too many enterprises represented part of the problem; the fact that some, being state-owned, were obliged to respond to the disparate goals of their respective governments, represented another source of difficulty; and the fact that a considerable part of the output of the various products lay in Australia and North America reduced the cartels' possibilities even further.

Blocked from pursuing stability by the cartel route, some buyers and sellers were trying to secure a measure of the stability through long-term contracts. In copper, the usefulness of that alternative was severely limited by the importance of the LME price. In aluminum, its relevance was largely confined to Japanese buyers, inasmuch as the rest of the industry was still vertically integrated. But in iron ore, the possibility of developing stability through long-term contracts at first seemed real.

As in oil, however, the stability imparted by long-term contracts in iron ore proved largely illusory. For a long time, contracts nominally covering a period of 10 to 30 years had been widely used among private parties in the industry. But the relationships between private buyers and sellers, such as those between the Swedish mines and the German steel mills or between the U.S. steelmakers and the U.S. ore companies, were long-term, highly stable affiliations. As state-owned enterprises took a more prominent role in the ore trade during the 1970s and as the oil industry provided its own striking illustrations of instability, the ore contracts also became less stable. Prices became subject to renegotiation every two years, and even the quantities foreseen in such contracts were constantly up for review and amendment.[21]

The unreliability of these long-term contracts led the affected parties to begin thinking about how to improve their security by other means. As we saw earlier, the response of the U.S. firms having so recently been burned by nationalizations, was to try to increase their security by reducing their foreign stake. Many U.S. firms, however, were not content simply to surrender their holdings in the developing countries and to fall back on the open market for their raw material requirements. In their efforts to recapture some of the stability that goes

Table 3.3. Sources of ores used by U.S. metal producers, 1970 and 1980 (in percent).

	1970	1980
Iron ore		
From United States	65.3	72.8
From threatened foreign sources[a]	15.5	8.4
From other foreign sources	19.2	18.8
Total	100.0	100.0
Copper ore[b]		
From United States	84.8	94.3
From threatened foreign sources[a]	13.0	4.3
From other foreign sources	2.2	1.4
Total	100.0	100.0
Bauxite[c]		
From United States	34.8	28.7
From threatened foreign sources[a]	55.4	39.8
From other foreign sources	9.8	31.5
Total	100.0	100.0

a. Threatened foreign sources include all sources in Latin America for all ores, plus the Philippines for copper ore. All African sources are also included, except Guinea in bauxite.

b. Including copper content of concentrate, matte, and blister.

c. Including alumina.

with vertical integration, U.S. firms began to invest in what they regarded as safer territories, such as the home territory of the United States, Australia, and Canada.

The effects of this retreat on the sourcing patterns of the U.S. metal producers were quite profound (see Table 3.3). Between 1970 and 1980, U.S. producers sharply reduced their imports of ores and other intermediate materials from the areas that appeared to be threatened, shifting to other sources. In iron ore and copper, the shift was mainly from Latin America to the United States. In bauxite, a product in which the element of security was less important to the metal producers, the shift was mainly from the Caribbean to other foreign sources.

In the case of copper, however, none of the measures to restore some degree of stability to the industry was enough to brighten the prospects of the metal producers. In this case, after pulling in their horns over much of the 1970s, many U.S. copper companies simply gave up as independent entities, allowing themselves to be taken over by oil companies with surplus cash. In the United States, the Atlantic Richfield Company bought Anaconda in 1977; the Standard Oil Company of Ohio (which is controlled by British Petroleum) bought Kennecott in 1981; the Standard Oil Company of California acquired 20 percent of Amax in 1975 and thereafter tried repeatedly to enlarge its holdings. In Australia, British Petroleum acquired 49 percent of the Olympic Dam copper property. And in Chile, Exxon bought the Disputada de las Condes mine. Although most oil companies soon came to regret their investments as costly and unprofitable, the effect was to reduce the risks in both the oil industry and the copper industry via the diversification route.[22]

Meanwhile, the problems of the developing countries in finding some way of stabilizing the export markets for their ores continued to be acute. The various reshuffles in such markets had not reduced the importance of such exports from the developing countries during the 1970s. On the contrary, between the years 1971–1973 and 1978–1980, developing countries managed to maintain their share of world exports of iron ore at 44 percent, to increase their share of copper exports from 56 percent to 63 percent, and to increase their share of aluminum exports from 9 to 13 percent.[23] To reduce their risks in the handling of these exports, state-owned enterprises in the developing countries undertook various experiments.

One such experiment was a proposal involving the governments of Jamaica, Trinidad-Tobago, and Mexico for the creation of a jointly owned aluminum complex; the proposals would link Caribbean bauxite with Mexican energy in a fully integrated structure.[24] But after years of effort, the project was abandoned in 1979: the political difficulties of putting together such a project proved, as usual, overwhelming.[25] Other, less ambitious efforts on the part of the state-owned enterprises have entailed government-to-government long-term purchase arrangements. But these have proved fragile and unreliable; and although such efforts will continue, they are not likely to provide the degree of market security that will leave the enterprises feeling comfortable.

State-owned enterprises also have been showing an increasing tolerance for creating joint ventures on their home territory with foreign enterprises. In such ventures, the foreign partner has typically provided any needed technology and has assumed the exporting function. As might be expected, the pattern has been especially common in aluminum, where the marketing risks for the unintegrated state-owned producers have been especially high. To be sure, such joint ventures occasionally appeared even in the 1960s. In aluminum, the state-owned Corporacion Venezolana de Guayana established a joint venture with Reynolds Metals in 1967; and the Norwegian government created a joint venture with Alcan in 1965. In the 1970s, however, aluminum ventures that entailed partnerships between state enterprises and foreign producers proliferated, appearing in Bahrain, Guinea, Dubai, Ghana, Venezuela, Iran, Jamaica, Brazil, and Italy.

Finally, even more hesitantly, some state-owned enterprises in the minerals industries have begun to think of reducing their marketing risks by setting up metal-processing facilities within some of their foreign markets. In one of the few realized cases of that sort, Zambia acquired a 50 percent interest in a French casting rod plant, creating an outlet for some of its copper.[26] In another, the Chilean state-owned enterprise Codelco acquired a 40 percent interest in a German fabricating plant.[27] Other possibilities also have been discussed.[28]

None of the efforts, however, has the scope and power that promise to bring stability to the minerals markets. Despite these incipient moves, the forces of diffusion that were at work in the 1960s and 1970s have not been greatly changed, and the prospects for stability seem slight.

Improving market efficiency. As the hope for stability has grown dimmer, some minds have turned to the possibility of reducing uncertainty by improving the efficiency of the world's markets and by introducing futures markets where these did not exist. As was noted in Chapter 2, that step had already been taken in oil, with the introduction of such public markets in London and New York. In minerals, the broadening of the LME metal markets and similar markets seemed to offer some possibilities.

It is worth noting, however, that the kind of added stability that an efficient futures market might provide would be much less than enough to satisfy the desires of most importing and exporting countries: their hopes, in the main, are for stability over a period of years. But such a market could conceivably reduce the short-term risks of both sides. Even that modest objective, however, seemed clouded by the experiences of the 1970s, when producing governments were exhibiting a disconcerting tendency at times to manipulate the public markets in the metals in which they had an interest, sometimes with a view of stampeding buyers to stock up on ores and metals.[29] To be sure, this is not a practice that is unknown when private producers predominate,[30] but the greater resources and greater immunities of governments suggest that the growth of state-owned enterprises may be accompanied by an increase in such operations.

In short, neither buyers nor sellers of metallic ores had reason to expect much price stability in international markets. On the other hand, sellers of ore no longer were in a position effectively to control supplies and prices, a situation that was reassuring from the viewpoint of importers such as the Japanese.

4

AMERICAN PRINCIPLES AND PRACTICES

Confronted with prospects of insecurity in a group of vitally important commodities, no two countries are likely to react in quite the same way. Each is the prisoner of its own history, operating mainly through a unique set of institutions and ideologies. History, therefore, offers plenty of clues to explain the country's policies with regard to the acquisition of critical materials and to suggest how the country is likely to act in the future.

A System of Governance

From Alexis de Tocqueville to Louis Hartz, a succession of perceptive scholars has commented on the remarkable consistency of the American people throughout their history in supporting a few basic ideas.[1] During the twentieth century, practically every grand pronouncement of a U.S. official body and every major institutional initiative of the U.S. government relating to raw materials have paid a required homage to the importance of maintaining an open competitive market. To that end, monopoly was to be avoided and the direct role of government was to remain severely limited. Even when the words in such grand pronouncements were merely rhetoric, they were a reflection of the values that the drafters thought they saw in the American people.

Where economic activities were concerned, however, American

political history has had another leitmotif, expressed eloquently by James Madison in *The Federalist* and embellished repeatedly by observers over nearly two centuries: the dominant role of special economic interests in shaping the nation's programs.[2] It has often been claimed that the role of such groups in U.S. political behavior is considerably stronger than in other mature industrial societies.[3] In speculating about the nature of future relations between the United States and Japan in the procurement of industrial materials, the critical question is whether U.S. behavior is likely to follow past patterns. On this point, scholars seem divided. For some, the seeming weaknesses and inconsistencies of the United States in confronting some of its most pressing international problems in the 1970s — such as the price of oil, the role of the dollar, the expropriation of U.S.-owned firms, nuclear proliferation, and human rights — are the result of deepseated forces in the society, difficult to change; their diagnoses suggest the continuation of a system of weak governments, strongly influenced by special interests. Others see the seeming weaknesses of the U.S. system during the 1970s, as one more manifestation of a cyclical phenomenon in American politics, reflecting an alternation between strong presidents and weak.[4] By this account, the Vietnam War and Watergate produced a revulsion against a strong executive and increased the power of the American institutions that were to act as checks and balances — the courts, the Congress, and the press. According to this view, there is no reason to assume that an era of stronger presidencies will not return. Yet there is ample reason to believe that even if a president were to emerge who was strong by U.S. standards, U.S. performance in the handling of its raw material problems would remain distinctly different from that of Japan.

One factor that separates the United States from other mature industrialized democracies is the way in which the twig was originally bent.[5] The upshot in the country's early years, as so many studies have pointed out, was a persistent emphasis on the diffusion of governmental authority. A considerable range of powers was allowed to remain in the states. In the federal structure, the powers of all three branches were intertwined and duplicated; in particular, the executive and the Congress were obliged to share their powers with each other and with the judiciary.[6]

The various explanations of the distinctive U.S. style of governance, however, appeal to other factors as well. Leaders in the U.S. economy never felt the special urgencies of Germany and Japan; the governments of these countries, according to the commonly held view, felt impelled to take a central role in helping their national business communities catch up with the competition. There was a brief period in the nineteenth century when the U.S. government did take some heroic initiatives in industrial policy, such as the state-supported building of the canals and the railroads.[7] But by the latter half of the century, it was clear that the Americans did not need help from a strong central government in order to acquire a leadership position in the industrial world. And although the idea of a strong central government surfaced from time to time thereafter, the preference for avoiding direct governmental operations in the economy continued to represent the dominant ideology.

The underlying tendency toward the fractionization of power, therefore, has survived through the decades, nurtured by the fact that national crises were few and that living standards were on the rise. When these conditions disappeared for a decade (in the 1930s) or when the country was in the midst of war (in the 1940s), the powers of the center temporarily grew — but not a great deal, and not for very long.[8] In the depths of the depression of the 1930s, the strongest president in modern U.S. history stood by, impotent, as the Supreme Court in a single decision overturned the country's key institution for its economic recovery, the National Recovery Act, on the grounds that it represented an unconstitutional delegation of power.[9] A few years later, in the midst of World War II and under the same president, Lord Keynes was so moved by the diffuse and uncertain process of decision making he saw in Washington as to remark acerbically to a group of American officials: "But you don't *have* a government in the ordinary sense of the word." Elaborating the point in his memoirs, Keynes noted that "the Administration, not being in control of the Congress, is not in a position to enter into commitments on anything."[10]

A few countries such as Australia and Canada have also structured their governments on the principle of the diffusion of power, but none quite so pervasively and aggressively as the United States. In the 1960s and 1970s the U.S. government adopted various innovations that pushed further in the direction that Lord Keynes discerned. During that period, numerous laws were enacted to give the public greater access to official records, to admit the public more widely to meetings of government agencies, and to increase the prolific rights of suit and appeal that have always existed in the American system of jurisprudence.[11] Although the beneficiaries of these laws were expected to be such "out" groups as ethnic minorities, environmental organizations, and the handicapped, the laws also enhanced the powers of various business and labor groups to shape the governmental process to their special needs.[12]

In the early 1980s the tendency of the U.S. political process to check, diffuse, and duplicate governmental powers seemed as virile as ever. By that time, various forces in the Congress had fashioned some added devices intended to rein in the executive. One of these was the proliferation of the congressional veto — that is, of provisions in various pieces of legislation that allowed the Congress to override actions of the executive taken in the execution of some given program. Provisions for such vetoes, almost unheard of a decade or two earlier, were rapidly increasing.[13] Another initiative, a group of bills still in the proposal stage, would vastly ease the burden of the public when challenging the decisions of agencies such as the Securities and Exchange Commission, the Federal Trade Commission, or the Environmental Protection Agency. These bills, by placing much heavier burdens of proof on the agencies whenever their decisions were being challenged in the courts, would weaken the power of the executive even more.[14]

The determined efforts of the American political process to check and diffuse the power of any government agency have been accompanied by an obvious decline in the strength of party affiliation and party discipline in national politics. This trend has been confirmed in numerous ways, including attitudinal studies of U.S. voters[15] and statistical analyses of the link between the party affiliation of congressmen and their electoral success.[16] As the party link has weakened, congressmen have turned more and more to acting as service bureaus for their local constituencies, rather than as members of a national party with common national goals.

Finally, the difficulty of maintaining a consistent direction in U.S. programs such as those in the field of industrial raw materials must also be attributed in part to the character of the country's bureaucracy. Unlike people in Britain, France, or Japan, the U.S. public has always resisted the idea of a tightly knit professional bureaucracy. U.S. values are not offended when a new president and his cabinet bring a fresh team of high administrators into office with them.[17] These administrators of the upper echelon, recruited for a temporary spell as bureau and department chiefs in Washington, typically share the usual ideological preferences of upper-income Americans, such as a desire to avoid monopoly and to limit the power of government.[18] Many, too, will be knowledgeable about Washington and politics. In other respects, however, they are a heterogeneous group, drawn from different professions, different schools, and different geographic origins. As a rule, they see themselves as members of a transitory coalition, not as committed bureaucrats who are part of the permanent machinery of government. Much more than their peers in other countries, they lack a sense of policy continuity, regard their personal values as important in the formulation of policy, and look on the promotion of policy as a competitive game played against others in the system.[19] The continuous changes in personnel and the wide variety of backgrounds in the bureaucracy have some advantages; for instance, they reduce the risks of bureaucratic rigidity and inflexibility. At the same time, consensual decision making and continuity of policy become extraordinarily difficult to achieve.

It is important to bear in mind, however, that such a loose-jointed governmental structure does not doom a government to inaction. Because the power to act in the name of the government resides in numerous officials and governmental bodies, and because a consensual process is not a prerequisite for national action, such a governmental apparatus can be quite activist in the conduct of its international affairs.

Sometimes the activism stems from a palpable emergency, such as the Japanese attack on Pearl Harbor, which has the effect of paralyzing the normal channels of consultation and debate. At other times the successful initiatives of a president occur in a period when the institutions that otherwise would check and balance are temporarily—but only temporarily—cowed. Most often, the activism stems from the fact that one force or another has managed to thread its way through the governing structure, avoiding the opposition and scoring a transitory victory on some narrow issue.

Because the structure of governance is so open, the forces that are bent on penetrating the system have numerous options. If they cannot penetrate the executive branch, they have a chance of moving the Congress; if not the Congress, then one of its committees; and if not the Congress or its committees, then the courts.[20] The preferred tactic—in sharp contrast, for example, to Japanese methods—is to circumvent the opposition, instead of dealing with it.[21]

Industry and government. The policies of the United States with regard to industrial materials have been shaped not only by the nature of its government but also by the structure of its industry. What is referred to as U.S. industry in fact includes a large group of firms that think of themselves as operating on a global scale.

The tendency to develop a global structure has been especially pronounced in the oil industry. In 1977, for instance, the U.S.-based multinational enterprises in the petroleum industry recorded 53 percent of their sales through foreign affiliates; and in the mining industries, U.S. firms reported 27 percent of their sales as taking place through foreign affiliates.[22] Much more than their Japanese competitors, American firms have relied on direct ownership and management of their foreign sources, and they typically have used their foreign facilities to serve not only the U.S. market but third-country markets as well.

As a rule, however, each major U.S. industry includes a number of important firms that operate principally in U.S. markets. Inescapably these domestic firms at times develop a set of preferences with respect to U.S. policy that are very different from those of their U.S.-based global competitors.

Even where differences do not exist within a U.S. industry between global firms and their domestic competitors, firms in the industry have considerable difficulty in concerting their policies. If a group of potential competitors sought to develop a joint approach to the importation of raw materials, for instance, their vulnerability under U.S. antitrust laws would be very high; and although antitrust authorities have winked at some potentially restrictive arrangements such as the Aramco partnership in Saudi Arabia or felt that they lacked the power to deal with them, the antitrust laws have typically held such arrangements in check. In the importation of raw materials, for instance, nothing like the collective purchasing arrangements that are common among Japanese materials users could survive in the U.S. legal environment.[23]

In speculating about the possibilities of future conflicts over the acquisition of raw materials, a key question is the interrelationship between U.S. firms and the U.S. government. The tendency of U.S. business as a class to hold the government at arm's length has been described and diagnosed at length in various studies.[24] Exceptions to the pattern occasionally appear: U.S. enterprises that depend heavily upon the military establishment for the bulk of their business or that face a palpable threat in foreign countries sometimes turn to their government for support. But these are notable exceptions to a strong contrary tendency.

U.S. enterprises that have developed a considerable stake in other countries have reasons other than ideology for holding their government at arm's length. Such enterprises are exposed to the uncoordinated and potentially conflicting commands of many governments; by maintaining too close a relationship with any one of them, a firm runs the risk of reducing its options in the handling of such conflicts. The activities of Aramco provide a dramatic illustration. During the oil crisis of 1973, Aramco responded with alacrity to the commands of the Saudi government to embargo the U.S. market and U.S. naval forces in nearby waters.[25] Gulf Oil's uninterrupted production activities in Angola and Mobil's activities in Libya, which have continued throughout several years of tension between the United States and those countries, also illustrate the possibilities of potential conflict. The fact that the principal enterprises of the United States respond to such diverse interests adds to the general sense of uncertainty that is so often attributed to U.S. behavior in international markets.

The air of uncertainty in U.S. behavior is, however, easily misinterpreted. Because the United States perceives itself as a global power, it dare not pursue any issue singlemindedly, not even an issue as important as that of securing access to industrial raw materials. If the U.S. government were considering an all-out effort to button down its supplies of raw materials from Latin America, for instance, it would have to weigh the effects of this effort on U.S. relations with suppliers from other areas, as well as on such disparate issues as the Law of the Sea negotiations and the negotiations for an international coffee agreement. U.S. decisions, therefore, characteristically entail a weighing and balancing of disparate factors that are far more complex than those confronting Japan. And that fact often imparts an air of inconsistency to U.S. actions.

Yet despite the fact that the U.S. government has seemed vacillating and inconsistent at times in the handling of its raw material problems over the decades, it has not failed to act. In various commodities there have been stockpiling programs, financing programs, export restrictions, import restrictions — all the trappings of an alert and responsive government. The problem, if problem there be, has been one of consistency and relevance in the stream of U.S. actions, rather than one of inaction.

Oil Shortages and Oil Policies

Because modern states regard an assured supply of oil as critical for their existence, U.S. oil policy represents an important testing ground of the way in which key national policies are formulated and implemented. The facts suggest that over the past century the U.S. government repeatedly identified some critical need with respect to its oil supplies and launched a program that seemed relevant to the goal. Characteristically, however, the objective of the program became modified or obscured in a short period of time. As the modifications piled up, the public objectives that had first inspired the program were submerged and the interests of one sector or another of U.S. industry became dominant.

Shortage after World War I. During much of the nineteenth century as the United States was developing its domestic industrial base and drawing primarily on domestic raw materials, its foreign interests were largely limited to promoting exports of those materials. By the early twentieth century, however, as the industrial strength of the U.S. economy became evident to Americans, the fear of opening up its manufacturing industries to foreign competition began to decline a little and declarations about the country's "manifest destiny" as a world power became commonplace.[26]

Immediately after World War I, the perception that the U.S. economy might be increasingly linked to a larger world economy found a sharp focus in the nation's first great spasm of worry over future supplies of crude oil.[27] Wartime procurement problems had aroused the worries of government officials over the limits of U.S. oil reserves, variously estimated as due for exhaustion in ten to twenty years. With the fear of a decline in the oil resources of the United States — indeed, of the Western Hemisphere as a whole — the stage was nicely set for a drive by U.S. oil firms to open up the Middle East and the Dutch East Indies for exploitation.

The events followed a pattern that would be repeated in later decades. The activist Democratic administration of Woodrow Wilson had identified a national problem of impending shortage, and had framed an acceptable American response — a response that supported the concept of open markets and the primacy of the private sector as the instrument for achieving the national objective. But the Wilson administration was succeeded in 1921 by the Republican administration of Warren G. Harding, bringing an inevitable interruption in policy continuity.

At first, it appeared that the idea of linking the U.S. oil industry to a world market for oil would not be a casualty of the change in administrations. The idea of supporting U.S. oil companies in their effort to secure a perch in the Middle East and the Dutch East Indies was in no way offensive to the ideology of the new administration, which was strongly probusiness in its orientation. But with the shift in administrations, the control over the tactics of the operation — and eventually the control over its strategic purpose — moved predictably from the government to the oil companies themselves. Even though the negotiations that followed would be mainly with the official representatives of Britain and France, the U.S. bureaucracy had neither the status nor the access to information about the oil industry that would allow it to take more than a supporting role.

Vast new findings in California in 1922 and Oklahoma in 1926 fundamentally altered the world's supply-demand balance from shortage to surplus.[28] The Soviet Union's reentry into world markets in the 1920s added to softness in prices.[29] The principal U.S. oil companies responded to the change very quickly. Instead of looking to the Middle East and the Dutch East Indies for more oil, the U.S. companies were now eager to join the British and the French in partnerships that could effectively control its supply. Despite the shift in objectives, the oil companies found that they could continue to count on the U.S. government for the occasional diplomatic support required.

In 1928 the efforts of the international companies bore fruit. The leading American, British, and French oil companies entered into a group of agreements that created an international oil cartel, an objective completely unrelated to the original purpose of the U.S. government's program and one substantially at variance with the ruling U.S. ideology.[30] Although the agreement never had the express support of the U.S. government, it would function over the next decade or two as a key element in a structure that controlled the world's oil supply and froze a division of the world's markets.

Such a cartel, however, could hardly have been effective for very long without bringing the U.S. domestic oil industry into the network. In 1929, therefore, the oil companies sought the views of the U.S. Department of the Interior on the feasibility of their organizing domestic producers to participate in the restrictive arrangements.[31] Eventually, the companies were advised that such and operation would be in violation of U.S. antitrust laws. At the same time, however, they were encouraged to support a program under which the individual states of the United States would control production in their respective territories. That approach had numerous political attractions. Although the arrangement was offensive to the concept of open markets, it was consistent with the principle of states' rights, a hoary and revered principle that was associated in the public mind with the diffusion and decentralization of power.

The inclusion of U.S. domestic producers, however, meant also that the multinational enterprises would have to share their position of strength with domestic oil interests. These consisted of hundreds of smaller firms spread over a dozen or more states, with considerable power in the state legislatures and in the U.S. Congress. In this period, as in those that were to follow, schemes of control that included U.S. production could not be administered without the support of these powerful interests. And the operations of the state-controlled pro-rationing system reflected that fact.[32]

Shortages in World War II. Another major stage in the history of U.S. oil policy began in 1943, when as a result of the war U.S. authorities were once more confronted with the seeming prospects of a long-term shortage of oil reserves in the Western Hemisphere.[33] Again, the authorities mobilized themselves to deal with that shortage.

In the abnormal atmosphere generated by wartime conditions, officials could entertain proposals that, in terms of U.S. ideological preferences, would ordinarily have been unthinkable. For instance, the ebullient and influential Secretary of the Interior, Harold F. Ickes, first made an effort to have the government acquire part or all of the equity of two middle-rank oil-producing companies in Saudi Arabia that were not signatories of the red-line agreement.[34] Dissuaded by the companies' hostile reactions, Ickes modified the proposal by stages until —predictably—it was finally withdrawn, making way in 1946 for a wholly private expansion of the Saudi fields.

However, official concern over the depletion of Western Hemisphere oil reserves had not disappeared altogether. Blocked from participating directly in the expansion of Saudi Arabian production, U.S. officials threw added support behind a proposed agreement between Britain and the United States that might oversee the orderly development of the world's scarce oil resources. The draft of such an agreement already existed at the time, having been negotiated in the wartime era with the support of the international oil companies. From the companies' viewpoint, such an agreement could be envisaged as a means of legitimating some of the market-stabilizing activities of the international oil cartel, including the control of production in periods of glut. That project, however, could not survive the return to a peaceful economy and a reversion to the country's ideological norms.

As usual, the shifts in official policy were influenced by the narrower objectives of special-interest groups. Most decisive in this process was the growth of opposition from the domestic oil producers to any international agreement that might put more controlling power in the hands of the U.S. government and the multinational oil companies. In a striking parallel to their political reaction of the late 1920s, the producers mobilized their political strength to resist the threat. For them, the controls exercised by the states over U.S. oil production were vastly preferable to a global mechanism, in which the influence of domestic producers might by greatly diluted.[35] As in the 1920s, therefore, the cycle of policy from 1943 to 1950 could be seen as one that began with the recognition of a pressing governmental objective and moved eventually to a resolution in which domestic interests played a leading role.

Old patterns and new interest groups. In the decades after 1950, the ideological preferences that had shaped and constrained the governmental role in oil remained remarkably stable. The processes of program formulation and implementation retained some of their longtime characteristics. A hyperactive bureaucracy, larger and more knowledgeable than its prewar counterpart, ground out a succession of proposals, some of which were actually launched. The oil industry, multinational and domestic, gradually restructured and reoriented those programs. New sources of political pressure also appeared, including notably some of the users of petroleum products, as well as organized groups that were trying to prevent the degradation of the environment.

The 1950s began with a series of events that could be construed as a reaffirmation of the fundamental ideological preferences of the United

States and of the dominance of large public goals over special-interest objectives. The Federal Trade Commission published an extraordinary report that described and condemned the international oil cartel,[36] and shortly thereafter the U.S. government instituted a grand jury investigation against the principal international oil companies, alleging antitrust violations.[37] In a separate action, the U.S. government brought suit against a number of oil companies from which it had been buying oil in connection with the Marshall Plan program for the economic recovery of Europe; the principal allegation in the suit was that a system of pricing existed that was anticompetitive in character.[38] In the same spirit, the government in 1954 used the occasion of the creation of a new Iran oil consortium to help a dozen so-called independent oil companies gain a foothold in the Middle East.

The early 1950s also was a period in which the U.S. government once again identified the existence of a long-run problem of materials scarcity. This time, the message was brought home in two different ways: by the resurgence of wartime concerns that arose during the Korean hostilities, and by the landmark 1952 report of the President's Material Policy Commission — the so-called Paley Commission report.[39] The Commission concluded: "In view of its future needs and limited resources, this nation should welcome crude imports, not place obstacles in their way. Tariffs on crude oil imports should therefore be held down, reduced, or eliminated, within the limits imposed by national security considerations." Notwithstanding the qualifying words of the final phrase, the commission's policy preferences were clear. What followed, however, was in the tradition of earlier episodes in the oil industry.[40]

The expansion of production by U.S. firms in the Middle East was proving to be a big success. The marginal costs of oil production in the Persian Gulf area, as the international oil companies were rapidly discovering, was proving extraordinarily low, much lower than U.S. production costs.[41] Accordingly, by the early 1950s five or six big international oil companies were landing the cheap oil of the Middle East in rapidly growing quantities in the east coast markets of the United States. Their imports were augmented by those of a new group of international oil companies that had managed to acquire their own sources of cheap foreign oil and that were even more eager than the majors to export some of it to their U.S. markets.

Not all U.S. oil producers, however, were willing or able to assume the costs and risks of penetrating these distant areas. Those that preferred to stay at home responded, as they had in times past, by marshaling their political support in Washington to restrict the flow of cheap oil to the United States.

The ensuing battle, which was already being waged in earnest during the last years of the Truman administration, faced the Eisenhower team in 1953. The new, Republican team, taking over after twenty years of Democratic dominance, felt no sense of commitment to the policies of the prior administration or to the findings of government-appointed groups such as the Paley Commission.

On the other hand, the complaints of domestic oil interests were a pressing political reality. The industry's argument was that the size of the U.S. oil reserves at any time depended on the size of the profits of producers operating in the country. On that assumption, the interests of the nation and the interests of the oil industry could easily be reconciled.

As a result, soon after Eisenhower assumed office, the scheme for the restriction of U.S. oil imports began to fall into place. At first, various devices were fashioned that might serve to restrict such imports without offending the general U.S. preference for open markets; for five years, efforts to control imports through a "voluntary" system were assiduously pursued. In 1959, however, the government established a system of mandatory import controls, overtly limiting the flow of cheap Middle East oil into the American market. The administration justified these restrictions on national security grounds, a position that provoked some opponents to deride the approach as a "drain America first" policy.

At that stage, however, it became evident that the ability to penetrate the loosely structured machinery of the U.S. government was not a power reserved for the multinational oil companies and their domestic competitors. Importers, users of oil, and environmentalists began to exert some influence. By 1973 the various interests that felt injured by the restrictive provisions of the oil import program had gradually chiseled away at the provisions until their restrictive effects had virtually disappeared.[42]

A few details of that process are worth recounting. Under U.S. norms, any windfalls associated with an import quota had to be fairly shared. Accordingly, with the institution of mandatory controls in 1959, all refiners of oil — whether or not the were dependent on imported oil — were included in the allocation of "import tickets." (Later, tickets would be allocated to petrochemical plants as well.) Those having no need for the tickets could sell them to those that did, thereby ensuring that all the tickets would be used. With industry interests satisfied by such means, the U.S. government process turned to satisfying some of the pressures from outside the industry. As the political implications of restricting oil from Mexico and Canada became apparent, the government was persuaded to exempt oil that was brought in overland. Later on, as the east coast felt the pinch of the restrictions on residual oil coming from Venezuela, special provisions were made for the importation of that product.

Other loopholes were punched into the system as new pressures appeared. A refinery established in the Virgin Islands acquired the extraordinary right to import as much crude oil as it liked and to ship its products freely to the U.S. mainland. Another refinery on the Texas-Mexico border was allowed to bring Mexican oil to the United States by tanker, ship the refined products back across the border to Mexico, then reenter them into the United States as "overland" oil.

Throughout the 1950s and 1960s, therefore, U.S. policy with regard to oil was altered by a process of accretion, an accumulation of little concessions to special interests. As the exceptions grew, it became clear that the gerrymandered system was proving easier on the importation of oil products than on the importation of crude oil itself. This was hardly surprising, inasmuch as one of the original objectives of the system had been to increase the profits of domestic crude oil producers. The U.S. economy found itself relying increasingly on refineries located outside the United States.[43] Even when that result became apparent in the late 1960s, the U.S. government failed to address the question of whether the development was consistent with U.S. interests.

With hindsight, it is evident that this was not the only problem building up during that period. The U.S. economy was also growing increasingly dependent on foreign oil. In 1950 the country imported about one-eighth of its petroleum needs; by 1970 the figure was up to nearly one-quarter; and by 1977 it had risen to nearly 50 percent.

At the same time, the overseas postion of the big international oil companies was being steadily weakened. The reasons for that weakening have already been recounted. They included the coming of age of politicians and technicians in the oil-exporting countries, a function of time, education, and improved communications; and their ability to reach out beyond the leading international oil companies to find new sources of technology and new outlets for their oil.[44] As a result, the position of the leading oil companies in the producing countries seemed imperiled.

At this stage, events provided a striking illustration of the extent to which U.S. foreign policy — especially the country's aspirations to lead a Western alliance — could inhibit any efforts to protect the country's more immediate interests. By the early 1970s, buoyed by a surging world demand for oil, Iran was pressing hard for larger profits, even if that required further increases in the price of crude oil. Inflation was becoming a grave problem in the United States and in Western Europe. The dollar, key currency in the world's trading system, was under siege. At the same time, U.S. leaders operated on the assumption that Iran's support was vital for the military and political security of the oil-exporting areas of the Middle East. In the clash between the two sets of interests, the political interests came out on top; the U.S. government bowed to the shah's demands.[45]

The 1973 crisis and its aftermath. Until 1973, serious analysts studying the place of oil in the security of the United States had usually been concerned with maintaining an adequate backlog of oil reserves in safe locations in the Western Hemisphere; to that end, they had at times urged that the importation of oil from the Middle East and other distant sources should be stepped up so that reserves in the Western Hemisphere could be conserved. That theme began to disappear in the 1950s, eventually to be replaced by a number of other policies and proposals.[46]

One group of policies was directed at the threat of sudden interruption. U.S. action against such a contingency was largely limited to two programs: building up a domestic stockpile, and sponsoring the creation of an International Energy Agency among a group of Western countries, whose aim would be to share scarce supplies with one another in the event of another crisis. In both programs, consistent with U.S. ideological preferences, the actual instruments for the sharing process were explicitly envisaged as the oil companies, rather than the governments themselves.[47]

As for the longer-run problems of vulnerability, these, too, were widely seen in the United States as best dealt with through the operations of the market. But the market was to be restrained or encouraged at various points, according to the powers of the numerous interest groups involved — the multinational oil companies, the domestic producers, the oil users, and the environmentalists. The details of that complex compromise have been analyzed ad nauseam in numerous sources.[48] It is enough to observe that the resolution of the conflicts proved generally consistent with the characteristics of earlier U.S. actions; that is to say, it entailed a progressive gerrymandering of a few clear principles until the general direction of the policy was almost totally obscured.

Because this phase of U.S. policy began in 1973 with an unprecedented run-up in oil prices, the oil users managed to place a freeze on the price of oil from existing domestic wells. With the prices of some domestic oil accordingly lower than that of foreign oil, there was a windfall to be had for those with access to such domestic oil. When there are windfalls to be distributed, U.S. practice is to find a form of distribution that minimizes the discretion of the bureaucrat and distributes the claims widely. In the 1950s, when access to cheap foreign oil would have provided a windfall, the U.S. government devised a system that spread the benefits of such access evenhandedly among the distributors and processors. In the 1970s, when access to cheap domestic oil provided the windfall, the principle of evenhandedness was even more extensively applied. By stages, a program was designed so that the average price that each domestic processor paid for its crude oil would be calculated as if all processors had equal access to old domestic oil.

The effect of this system, to be sure, was to lower the price of U.S. oil below the world price, and to increase U.S. consumption at a time when the paramount objective of U.S. policy seemed exactly the opposite. But large portions of the American public could explain away their unease by insisting that the oil shortage was a fraud, artificially created by the big oil companies or the federal government.[49] The other interests that had played so large a role in the shaping of oil policy in prior periods were still very much in the picture. The multinationals were suddenly enjoying unprecedented profits, partly because of an increase in the value of inventories and partly because of a widening in margins all through the chain of production and distribution. A modest windfall tax imposed in 1979 left them with the bulk of their profits. The domestic oil and gas interests had an obvious interest in freeing themselves from the restraints of price controls; they began to achieve this objective in 1975, when it was agreed that the price of domestic oil would be decontrolled by stages, and went a little further in 1978 when the price of domestic gas was allowed to begin floating upward. Both these groups could work for their objectives with a relatively easy mind, secure in the recognition that higher prices and higher profits meant lower aggregate consumption of oil and lower reliance in the short run on the oil of the Middle East.

Seen through the eyes of the American participants, the outcome was typical of the U.S. political process. Seen through the eyes of other governments, such as the Japanese or the French, the outcome was close to incomprehensible. Unlike many other countries concerned with increasing the security of their foreign oil supplies, the United States did not seriously contemplate mobilizing the economic power latent in the world's needs for U.S. exports of food, technology, and capital. The fact is, of course, that the U.S. government could not have taken control of such exports for international bargaining, without bitter opposition from within the U.S. political structure itself.

There was a second sense in which the outcome seemed typically American. By the early 1980s, considerable progress had been made toward reducing the country's dependence on imported oil, at least in the short run. From peak daily imports of over nine million barrels a day, the country had reduced its daily needs to four of five million barrels, a response induced largely by a drop in total consumption. But the reduced dependence on imported oil was also being achieved in part by drawing on scarce and expensive U.S. oil supplies, hence by a policy of exhausting U.S. oil reserves as rapidly as possible. That response might conceivably be justified if the problem could be seen as mainly one of managing a short-term transition from the reliance on Middle East oil to other energy sources. Practically all the analyses available to the U.S. government, however, saw the problem of dependence as being much more prolonged. A resumption of rapid economic growth, a decline in the relative price of oil, or an eruption in the Middle East could plunge the U.S. economy once more into difficulty.

By 1981, when a new Republican administration took office, discussions of long-run vulnerability were rarely heard. In early 1982, when a number of U.S. firms responded to a dip in crude oil prices by abandoning their long-term projects for developing synfuels and shale oil, the official U.S. establishment was ostentatiously mute; even a basic national decision of these dimensions, according to the administration's ideology, was one to be left in the hands of the private sector.

Only the problem of short-term vulnerability still commanded much attention; and even on that subject, one could detect a flagging official interest. The government stockpile by this time had been built up to about 300 million barrels, about one-third of its goal. But as crude oil prices weakened and declined during 1982, the Reagan administration reacted in the predictable American pattern. The objective of developing a cushion against a new oil crisis was pushed aside in favor of cutting governmental expenditures. Despite the obvious risks, the administration sharply reduced the rate at which oil was being acquired for the stockpile.

In other ways, too, the problem of vulnerability slipped further on the political agenda. The new administration, even more firmly devoted than its predecessors to the principle of limiting the direct operational role of government, pruned back the government's contributions to the development of alternative sources of energy. At the same time, stimulated partly by ideology and partly by the well-focused pressures of various interest groups, the administration relaxed many of the environmental and other restraints that might incidentally have slowed the exhaustion of safe supplies of oil. By 1982 the administration seemed agreed on a policy of encouraging the private sector to tap at the earliest possible date the one remaining oil reserve of the country — namely, the areas of the continental shelf.[50] Evidently it would take another great emergency before the nation could shift its attention back to the problem of increasing the long-term security of its energy supplies.

Mining and Metals

An analysis of U.S. policies with regard to the mining and metals industries adds little that has not already been illustrated by the case of oil. Spasms of worry on the part of the government have produced brief flurries of official action to increase the security of the supply of metal ores. The U.S. government has at various times given international support to one country or another, partly on the grounds that the country was the source of some critical mineral. The Reagan administration, for instance, displayed special warmth to South Africa, contending that it was an important source of manganese and chrome. But such policies have been sporadic and ephemeral, rarely outlasting a single presidential administration.

Only in one significant respect has the interplay of these forces in the metals and minerals industries differed from that in oil: the political power of the various metals and minerals industries has been much more limited. As a result, the metals and minerals industries have not had anything like the oil industry's success in obtaining special exemptions from major governmental policies such as antitrust; nor have they been as successful in resisting ad hoc pressures from government agencies and consumer groups that have been adverse to industry interests.

The open competitive market. As we saw in Chapter 3, the metals and mining industries have shown a persistent tendency to develop near-monopolies, strong oligopolies, and cartels — a tendency that was bound from time to time to evoke the displeasure of the U.S. government. The government's distaste for international cartels was all of a piece with its support for the concept of open international markets. That distaste was voiced sporadically in the 1920s,[51] and vigorously in the 1930s; the launching of the congressional Temporary National Economic Committee in 1938 was the opening gun for a great reaffirmation of the American commitment to the antitrust approach.[52] In the committee's twenty thousand pages of testimony and forty-three monographs, the restrictive arrangements of the metals and mining industries occupied a prominent place. In the decade that followed, several major antitrust cases in the mining and metals industries underscored the importance of that sentiment.[53]

Metals and minerals figured prominently in other U.S. policies that were consistent with the open-market concept. After World War II, the government was prepared through its Export-Import Bank and its Overseas Private Investment Corporation to help finance and guarantee foreign investments of U.S. enterprises, including those in metals and mining.[54] In this respect, the United States may have appeared no different from many other countries, including Japan, that were prepared to bolster their foreign sources of supply through vigorous government action. But critical differences did exist, suggesting much less clarity of purpose or sense of urgency in the U.S. case. For one thing, until quite recently oil production was omitted from these U.S. programs, presumably out of deference to the country's domestic producers. Moreover, the lending and guaranteeing facilities were not channeled by any set of strong priorities or restraints; they were available to all eligible applicants, as defined by law and regulation, according to the initiatives of the applicants.[55]

The spirit of the open market, unguided for the most part except by the preferences of private enterprises, ran as a consistent thread through the various reports on industrial raw materials that were produced in the years after World War II. Although the Paley Commission's 1952 report was clear on the gravity of increasing shortages of metals and minerals for the United States, its principal remedy was largely consistent with the traditional American preference for the open-market approach; firms were urged to step up their development projects in foreign countries. Two years later, the wider-ranging Commission on Foreign Economic Policy—dubbed the Randall Commission—endorsed open markets and greater overseas investment as the preferred policies for ensuring an adequate supply of raw materials.[56] In the early 1970s, as the specter of raw materials shortages reappeared in a more acute form, national pronouncements about the general policy of the United States again stressed a preference for open competitive markets. In 1973 a National Commission on Materials Policy, which had been created by President Nixon, endorsed essentially the same propositions as the ones the Paley Commission had adopted two decades earlier.[57]

The commitment of the U.S. government to the open-market concept was not wholly confined to declarations and reports. In the first flush of postwar planning, the government had grudgingly acknowledged the possibility that in special circumstances commodity agreements among governments might be justified.[58] In actual practice, however, the country persistently resisted the proposals of other nations for the creation of such commodity agreements. For thirty years following World War II, a succession of major initiatives were pressed in United Nations agencies and elsewhere for agreements that would stabilize prices and production in the various minerals.[59] Tactical considerations sometimes led the U.S. delegations not to resist these proposals head on; but with occasional quixotic exceptions, the characteristic U.S. position ranged from quiet footdragging to outright opposition.[60] And in the early 1980s, when other governments sought to place restrictions on the production of minerals in the context of the proposed Law of the Sea Treaty, the U.S. government resisted those restrictions as long as it safely could; only its strong desire to nail down the other treaty provisions, such as assured access for its navy in various coastal waters, led the U.S. government finally to bend its position.[61]

The durability of the U.S. preference for limiting the role of government in commodity markets was put to a special test between 1973 and 1976, a time of turmoil in the raw material markets. For some years previously, various governments in Latin America and Africa had been expropriating mining properties owned by foreign firms, and in the mid-1970s the practice continued at an accelerated rate. These disturbing events produced no resolute counteraction from the United States since the inhibitions created by the multiplicity of U.S. foreign policy objectives could be counted on to deflect any effective reaction. Some U.S. observers at the time quailed at the specter of collusive cartels depriving the U.S. economy of needed resources;[62] but U.S. policy makers continued to place their faith in the durability of private enterprise and the unwisdom of direct governmental involvement in the world's commodity markets.[63] The only significant exception to that principle, it seemed, was a willingness to enlarge the country's program for stockpiling essential minerals.

Stockpile policies and special interests. Proposals to stockpile have been the standard U.S. response to periodic fears that the country might be facing a shortage of key minerals. But usually, once the executive branch of the U.S. government has identified the problem of scarcity and proposed the stockpile solution, it has been obliged to make peace with a series of special interests. As a result, in a familiar and characteristic sequence, the government has soon appeared to lose sight of any stockpile program that it has initiated, rapidly becoming diverted from its original security objectives.

Although minerals specialists were worrying about national shortages as early as 1921, the first stockpile legislation was not enacted until 1939.[64] In a succession of measures enacted between 1939 and 1946, the domestic mining industry demonstrated that it could impose "buy American" requirements on a reluctant government, thus turning the stockpile program into one for supporting the industry. But it did not have the political clout completely to prevent purchases from foreign sources or sales from the stockpile.[65]

Almost as soon as World War II ended, however, the nation's interest in developing adequate stockpiles of strategic materials began to evaporate. The cold war and the Korean War provided the atmosphere for a brief encore for activist policies. These episodes allowed the U.S. government to enter into numerous substantial commitments for increasing the production of key minerals, including loans, guarantees, and purchase contracts.[66] And because the domestic industry could not quite muster the political power to block foreign purchases, slightly more than half of the actual expenditures took place abroad.

By 1953 the government's policy makers had the benefit of the Paley Commission's detailed studies of the prospects for increasing dependency on the part of the U.S. economy, as well as a detailed set of policy recommendations. The commission's report included proposals for a permanent stockpiling program, secondary stockpiles, mothballed production facilities, and stand-by technologies for processing low-grade ores in an emergency.

But under the U.S. system of governance, none of this proffered advice could survive the change in administration from Truman to Eisenhower. The new administration's disposition to give domestic oil producers higher profits was matched by a willingness to respond more readily to the complaints of the domestic mining industry. Within a year, the new administration had announced a revised stockpile policy, one that would give preference to purchases of "metals and minerals of domestic origin."[67] To strengthen the effects of that policy, the government undertook to negotiate a number of "voluntary" agreements with exporting countries, aimed at reducing their exports; under the threat of increased U.S. import restrictions, Canada, Mexico, Peru, Australia, and others were persuaded to place restrictions of various sorts on their exports of metals. From 1954 to 1958, the nation's stockpile purchases provided a bonanza for the domestic lead and zinc industry, which sold almost half its production to the stockpile.[68]

It was during this period, too, that the practice of using the stockpile for short-term tactical political purposes began to take hold as a regular practice. To help the overseas subsidiaries of U.S. mining firms and to throw a bone to the agricultural lobby, surplus U.S. agricultural commodities were bartered for foreign metals.[69] To keep in operation some fabricating plants that were temporarily cut off from their supplies of copper metal, supplies from the stockpile were diverted. All told, however, the pressures of the domestic industry for government support proved powerful enough, so that by the end of the 1950s, with the close of the Eisenhower administration, the country's stockpiles were swollen.[70]

The years that followed produced a succession of mercurial shifts in stockpile management; for brief periods, those shifts bore some relation to the asserted purposes of the stockpiles, but more often they reflected efforts to respond to some ephemeral political pressure.

The 1960s opened with President Kennedy's decision to bow to the pressures of the lead and zinc lobby by providing subsidies to the industry. But shortly thereafter the administration was selling from the stockpiles in order to bring them down to levels that could be justified on security grounds. Later, when the problems of the Vietnam War took hold, stockpile sales were used to dampen upward price pressures and to increase government revenues. By this time, the link between the stockpiles and the security interests of the United States had been greatly attenuated.

The raw material shortages that occurred in the first half of the 1970s, however, restored the connection between national security and industrial materials. The Nixon administration's study of the nation's raw materials situation in 1973 retraced the ground that the Paley report had covered nearly twenty years earlier.[71] The results of that study appeared just as the world seemed confronted with a great wave of material shortages, accompanied and exacerbated by the formation of a series of multinational cartels in hard minerals. The report nevertheless largely endorsed the fundamental propositions of the Paley report, with its emphasis on keeping the market open to imports while encouraging the expansion of domestic production. Similar themes were repeated in a 1976 study, which was launched as the developing countries formed their various international organizations to restrict exports of copper, aluminum, and iron ore.[72] Not surprisingly, the government turned back to stockpiles as its means for dealing with interruptions in supply, and authorized a new build-up of the depleted stocks. By 1976 the pattern of minerals held in official stockpiles was beginning to show some rough-and-ready relationship to the country's perceived supply risks; on hand, for instance, were five years' worth or more of chromite, cobalt, tungsten, and manganese, together with somewhat lesser quantities of tin, mercury, and platinum, and less than a year's supply of lead, zinc, and copper.[73]

With the advent of the Reagan administration, however, there were new affirmations that the stockpiles would be used for any purpose the government found useful, whether or not it related to the original need. In 1982, in a characteristic manifestation of U.S. governmental style, the president directed the stockpile authorities to buy large quantities of Jamaica's bauxite.[74] The purchase had nothing to do with stockpile objectives; its purpose was to bolster the position of a friendly government. Predictably, most of the bureaucratic apparatus was bypassed in the making of the decision. Equally predictably, the decision aroused opposition in some quarters of the Congress, with threats to overturn the presidential initiative. The machinery of government, it appeared, was still running in its usual patterns.

Reprise

There is more reaffirmation than revelation in this account of U.S. policies. Other scholars, working in somewhat different contexts, have already tracked over some of the ground covered here and have drawn compatible conclusions.[75] During the past few decades, official and unofficial bodies have produced a number of thoughtful studies regarding the long-run problems of securing sources of raw materials. Such studies have usually recognized the need not only to develop but also to conserve supplies in safe areas. That conclusion has generally pointed to a policy that encouraged the development and use of foreign supplies while ensuring that the domestic industry retained some spark of vitality. But true to U.S. ideological preferences, proposals for a direct operating role for U.S. agencies have been rare, and those that have been made have typically suffered a quick death. As a result, maintaining adequate reserves in safe places has been left largely to the discretion of the private sector. Private firms, however, have had no responsibility and no incentive to work toward any such objective. Their aim has been to survive and prosper in industries in which the risks are increasing and in which the pricing structures have become increasingly insecure.

U.S. government policy in the field of industrial materials, it is true, has not been wholly passive. Government initiatives have appeared sporadically to deal with the threat of acute problems of shortage in the near future. But the programs have usually been carefully circumscribed by the country's ideological preferences for avoiding a direct operational role on the part of government. Eventually, the actions taken under the authority of such programs have been shaped largely by the outcome of unremitting skirmishes among special interests. Under the U.S. system, these warring interests have had neither the inclination nor the need to trade off their conflicting objectives in an agreed-upon long-run program bearing some relation to national needs.

5

JAPAN'S INSTITUTIONS AND PRACTICES

In its policies toward the acquisition of raw materials during the past thirty years, Japan has differed from the United States in one critical respect. There have been struggles and debates inside the country over its policies, as well as occasional false starts and outright errors. But the policies that have been selected have followed a coherent line and have been more or less responsive to the country's needs. At first, Japan's emphasis was on securing its raw materials at the lowest possible prices. In the 1970s, security of supply became a major consideration, especially with regard to oil. In the 1980s, in response to the country's improving procurement capabilities, Japan has begun to balance security with efficiency in an effort to respond to both objectives.

During most of Japan's modern history, the country's concern about the availability of key industrial materials has been understandable enough. With few raw materials of its own, it has always had to rely heavily on foreign sources. As a latecomer to the rank of industrialized nations, it has had to confront the entrenched positions abroad of enterprises from other countries. Besides, in viewing the likely behavior of these foreign-owned enterprises, the Japanese have typically assumed that there was a high degree of concordance and collaboration between the enterprises and their respective governments, a perception that has heightened Japan's sense of exposure to foreign political pressures.

Japan's policies and practices with regard to industrial raw materials, however, were not simply the result of its perceptions of high risk. Whether because of the country's distinctive position as a have-not latecomer or because of cultural factors that had their roots elsewhere, Japan has formulated and executed its policies through a set of institutuions different in critical respects from those of the United States.

The Japanese System

Over the past few decades, a hoard of analysts have exposed and dissected the political, social, and economic structure of Japan, hoping to understand the process that has produced the country's phenomenal economic performance.[1] For once, the studies of the academic community have shown considerable agreement, albeit with a few important differences in interpretation yet to be resolved.

A *system of governance.* Japan, like the United States, is a practicing democracy, in which political power is well dispersed. Although the country has been governed by only one party since the peace treaty following World War II, that party is actually a coalition of various rival factions, whose competitive strength within the party rests on their ability to command the popular vote. And although the minority parties have been unable to take power, they have not been wholly without influence upon governmental policy.[2] An independent press and an autonomous judiciary fill out the picture of a practicing democracy.[3]

There is another fundamental respect in which Japan and the United States present striking similarities. Competitive marketing plays a very considerable role in the economies of both countries. Although the Japanese government engages in price control more readily than its U.S. counterpart, price competition among Japanese producers is endemic.[4] Advertising, too, plays a vital role in domestic marketing.[5] And as in the United States, the formation of new business ventures and the bankruptcy of existing ventures are commonplace.[6]

Yet despite these basic similarities, Japan's culture and system of governance represent in numerous fundamental ways the antithesis of their American counterparts. Those differences, extensive and deep-rooted, produce differences in style and method that sharply distinguish the strategy and operations of the two countries.

Perhaps the most important difference lies in the fact that industry organizations and governmental agencies play a much more direct role in the Japanese economy than in the economy of the United States.[7]

These organizations introduce a measure of coordination and control in Japan that is critical in the country's relations with foreigners. The concept of "administrative guidance" by the government, a concept offensive to the U.S. culture, is a firmly established part of Japan's economic environment.[8] Without involving the authority of any explicit law, the Japanese government in August 1979 suddenly imposed "guidelines" on its trading companies that prevented them from completing lucrative deals for the importation of spot oil.[9] In another manifestation of its power, the government compelled the giant Mitsui interests to retain a foothold in a vast Iranian petrochemicals enterprise long after the firm was eager to withdraw.[10]

This aspect of the Japanese economy has been grossly parodied in the American and European press, creating the basis for the notorious Japan Incorporated metaphor. Japanese firms on occasion can be fractious and willful, bitterly resisting the suggestions of government and striking out on an independent course. Nevertheless, those episodes are less common with respect to foreign issues than domestic ones; and they are carried out by the public and private disputants in a spirit which suggests that each side recognizes its need for the other over the long run.

For various reasons, the inherent capacity of Japan's government to guide its enterprises on a sustained basis is far greater than that of the U.S. government. One of the more obvious reasons is the fact that Japan is a parliamentary democracy, hence a democracy that has greater similarities to Great Britain or France than to the United States. The power to govern the domestic economy lies much more firmly in the executive branch and its bureaucracy than in the case of the United States. The Japanese parliament and courts have nothing like the capacity of the U.S. Congress and courts to duplicate the executive's authority or to veto the executive's actions.

The power, however, is in the executive branch and its bureaucracy as a whole, not in the person of the prime minister. One factor that limits the power of the prime minister and other members of the cabinet is the competence and cohesiveness of the bureaucracy. This is no "government of strangers," such as the United States produces, periodically dismantled and reconstituted in a vast house-cleaning of key positions, as political leaders come and go. It is a professional bureaucracy, operated on the usual Japanese principles of recruitment by merit and of lifetime tenure in a single ministry or agency. Its members normally take their posts on the basis of a long weeding-out process that begins in middle school, a process that channels the most promising aspirants through a few prestigious universities into government service.[11] In each ministry, the entering group in any year is indoctrinated and socialized as a class, retaining its group identity throughout the professional lives of its members. Ministers rely upon these professionals to a degree that is only infrequently matched in the United States.[12] In American terms, the Japanese have unequivocally chosen the Hamiltonian tradition over the Jacksonian.

Although the Japanese bureaucracy exercises considerable power, it is restrained by a potent factor that has no counterpart in the U.S. bureaucratic process. This is the pronounced tendency of Japanese society, much advertised and widely documented, to reach decisions by building a national consensus.[13] That generalization, however, can easily be misunderstood and misinterpreted. Some observers insist, for instance, that the consensus which is so commonly identified with the Japanese political process is usually an agreement among elites, rather than agreement at the grass roots. Moreover, the agreement is not achieved without bitter struggles in the system.[14] Indeed, decision making inside the Japanese government shares many characteristics with the chaotic process that has been so well described for the United States.[15] The rivalries, animosities, and alliances that are the bread and butter of Washington bureaucratic politics have fairly close counterparts in Tokyo, but with one profound difference: whereas the common strategy of the strangers who make up the U.S. government is to try to avoid and circumvent the opposition, the Japanese approach is to find a process of decision making in which all the affected parties have participated. That approach may prolong the decision-making process endlessly. If eventual consensus is ever achieved, it may be the result of wearing down the opposition or adopting a compromise that seems extraordinarily ambiguous to outsiders; but it is ordinarily indispensable for Japanese action.[16] In this sense, one might say that the Japanese government behaves rather like the highly socialized U.S. Senate, whose members are aware that they must live with one another over the long pull, and not in the least like the U.S. government as a whole.

The difference between the Japanese and American governments in this aspect of their decision making is consistent and pervasive. It is found not only in the relations of the executive to other branches of the government, but also in relations between the different parts of the executive branch, and among the various divisions within ministries or agencies. The same characteristic is found within individual business firms in Japan.[17] In all likelihood, that trait is linked inseparably to the other characteristic that distinguishes Japanese from U.S. processes — namely, the much greater stability in the positions of institutions and individuals in Japanese structures. With stability of the various participants assured, none can as readily afford to win an isolated decision through evasive action.

Business and government. The nature of the interactions between Japan's government agencies and the country's business institutions has been influenced by more than the general style of Japan's system of governance. Economic historians are almost certainly right in attributing the close ties between business and government in part to the latecomer status of Japan as an industrializing power.[18] By the time Japan was ready to launch modern industries, the technology was already in the hands of other countries; by the time her firms were searching abroad for secure sources of oil and minerals, the enterprises of the United States and Europe had already staked out claims to the most obvious sources in Asia, Africa, and Latin America. It seemed almost inevitable, therefore, that Japanese business should summon up the help of government in overcoming its latecomer status.

That late start was probably instrumental also in helping to give the Japanese enterprise a distinctive strategy as it attempted to penetrate foreign markets and foreign sources of materials. Unlike the Americans, Japanese firms until quite recently had made few direct investments in raw materials in foreign countries; and even when they invested, they rarely sought to manage the foreign properties in which they had a financial stake. On the other hand, free of the restraints imposed by antitrust statutes, the Japanese have commonly organized their buying in any country through joint arrangements with other Japanese firms, including consortia, trading houses, and chosen lead firms. And they have frequently been assisted in such joint buying arrangements by initiatives from the government side.

The strategies of Japanese firms in acquiring overseas sources of raw materials have also been affected by the Japanese government's central role in the financing of Japanese business. By U.S. standards, big business in Japan is burdened with a remarkably high level of debt, of which an unusually large proportion is either official in origin or is subject to official guidance. In the 1975–1979 period, for instance, a little over 40 percent of the funds of Japanese corporations came from bank credit, including credit extended by official banking institutions or by private banks. Such credit, whether from public or private banking sources, was much influenced by governmental policy such as the Bank of Japan's practice of "window guidance" — that is, its practice of suggesting to lending banks where their added loans should be directed.[19] In the United States, in the same period, corporations drew about 25 percent of their funds from bank borrowing and bonds, of which hardly any were governmental.[20]

More narrowly, the evidence indicates that the capital-intensive raw materials industries are especially affected by the differences. One study covering the middle 1970s compared the capital structure of eight Japanese nonferrous metal firms with five U.S. firms in the same industries. In the case of the Japanese firms, about 90 percent of the capital came from debt, whereas the comparable figure for the U.S. firms was in the neighborhood of 50 percent.[21]

The government's influence on business policy does not depend on the banking channel alone. The process is helped by the private sector's respect for the position and capacity of the governmental bureaucracy. (The fact that the movement of former government officials to business is referred to as *amakudari* — literally, descending from heaven — is a telling sign of the relationship.) It is helped as well by a highly articulated set of institutions. On the government side, the much celebrated Ministry of International Trade and Investment (MITI) has been the key entity; on the business side, the almost equally well-known Federation of Economic Organizations, the Keidanren, has been the pivotal organization.

The Keidanren functions as the supreme coordinating body of big business in Japan. Although it is an organization for private business, the Keidanren's corporate membership also includes public and quasi-public corporations such as the Japan National Railways, the Japan Development Bank, and the Bank of Japan. Its elaborate staff is buttressed by an impressive array of several hundred prominent corporation executives, mostly presidents and board chairmen, who serve as directors. Its activities run a wide gamut, but consultation with the government constitutes the central function.[22]

Formal manifestations of some of the results of this consultation process have appeared periodically in the reports of so-called deliberation councils, bodies made up of prestigious senior figures from private industry, government enterprise, trade associations, and universities. Councils of this sort have been responsible for producing a series of reports, defining the goals to be achieved and the programs to be pursued in their achievement.[23]

As was noted earlier, similar reports have been produced sporadically by prestigious commissions in the United States, but there has been a critical difference in the role that such reports have played in the two societies. The U.S. reports have been largely hortatory and educational, whereas the Japanese reports have defined a framework in which Japanese business and government have been expected to act. The framework has legitimated the subsequent behavior of Japanese government agencies and credit institutions in selecting specific projects and choosing specific firms for special support.

The fact still remains that powerful and strong-willed business executives in Japan can sometimes resist the pressures of the bureaucracy to conform to official views. In the 1960s the resistance of Japan's automobile industry to MITI's attempts to force mergers was resolute and successful; so, too, was the resistance of Japan's mainframe computer producers to similar MITI attempts in the 1970s.[24] But as the managing director of Nippon Oil Company recently observed, "We cannot ignore what MITI has to say."[25]

The element of cooperation has characteristically been even stronger on issues in which foreign economies are to be confronted. The cooperation between government and enterprise in foreign trade and investment manifests itself in numerous ways. Where a special entrepreneurial push from the government has seemed useful, MITI has had no great difficulty in securing the needed authority to create a new publicly controlled enterprise. Accordingly, various public organizations that have no counterpart in the United States—some owned by the state, some ambiguously endowed with responsibility for serving the public interest—have acted to coordinate private actions with public objectives.[26] In addition, specialized official lending institutions, operating on a very large scale, have funneled credit to the private sector on a highly selective basis for closely targeted purposes.[27] In the field of industrial raw materials, the distinctive institutions and practices have produced a set of policies and programs that are starkly different from those of the United States.

The Case of Oil

To understand how the Japanese have approached the problem of access to oil in recent years, one needs to know something of the overwhelmingly vital role that oil has played at critical points in Japan's modern history. The fact that Japan imports practically all of that basic commodity only begins to tell the story. The fact that until very recently most of that oil has been imported under the control of foreign companies suggests a little more. What has to be recalled in addition is that throughout most of the country's modern history, Japan's efforts to gain direct access to foreign oil were blocked by the commanding position of U.S. and British companies, a fact that hobbled Japan in its efforts to expand into Asia in the 1930s and that greatly increased the country's difficulties during World War II. Oil, from the Japanese viewpoint, was not just another basic commodity; it was the country's historic Achilles' heel.

Origins of the policy. Japan's dependence on foreign oil goes back to the nineteenth century, when Standard Oil of New York (later Socony Vacuum, later still Mobil) began exporting to Japan from the United States and the Dutch East Indies.[28] By 1928 the principal international oil companies of the world — none of them Japanese — had developed a set of alliances through which they effectively controlled the world trade in oil. By that time, Exxon (then the Standard Oil Company of New Jersey) and Mobil, together with the British-Dutch combination of Royal Dutch Shell, were securely in control of the principal sources of crude oil and the principal refineries in Japan's part of the world. From the time Japan seized Manchuria in 1931 until it attacked Pearl Harbor ten years later, the country was engaged in a continuous effort to gain some measure of control over the refineries and oil supplies on which its national economy so heavily depended.

For the most part, Japan's efforts were thwarted. As late as 1939, Japanese interests controlled only a tiny fraction of the oil that the country consumed; and practically all of the country's imports of crude oil and oil products came from the Dutch East Indies or from the west coast of the United States. To make matters worse, there were signs from time to time during these difficult decades that the international oil companies were working hand in glove with their respective governments to frustrate Japan's objectives. When in 1934 Japan sought to monopolize the refining and distribution of oil and oil products in its puppet state of Manchukuo, the Japanese government was faced with "rhetorical thunder" from London and Washington.[29] At about the same time, Japan began to impose regulations on its home territory in order to generate an indigenous capacity for oil refining and a national oil stockpile; in reaction, the country had to reckon with the oil companies' hints of a retaliatory embargo and with sporadic diplomatic protests from the United States and Britain.

The tension that this dependence created can easily be imagined. Traditionally, the naval strategic planning of Japan tended to identify the United States as the principal hypothetical enemy.[30] After Japan seized Manchuria in 1931 and from time to time in the decade that followed, discussions in the West of the possibility of embargoing oil to Japan seemed to confirm Japan's vulnerability.[31]

The work of scholars since that time strongly suggests that the seeming teamwork of the U.S. oil companies and the U.S. Department of State during the middle 1930s was mainly the result of different interests that sometimes offered the opportunity for joint action. The diplomats were consumed with the importance of the Open Door principle, whereas the oil companies had their eyes mainly on the processing and selling of oil products. Because of the differences in perspective, the oil companies could not always count on diplomatic support when they felt they needed it; such support turned out to be sporadic and episodic, its timing, tone, and content being influenced by larger developments in world politics.

There were other signs at the time that, in facing the United States, Japan was not exactly confronting a monolith. In 1934 when Stanvac, Texas Oil, and Shell Oil threatened to pull their subsidiaries out of Manchuria in reaction to pressures from the Manchurian monopoly, Standard Oil of California and Union Oil — two companies regarded in the 1930s as "independents" — offered to fill their shoes.[32] But even if the Japanese were aware of the less-than-total cohesion of the U.S. companies and the U.S. government, the recognition probably offered only cold comfort.

Besides, as prewar tensions built up in the latter 1930s, the oil companies and their respective governments moved closer together. By that time, the main concern of the United States and its European allies was to avoid goading Japan into an attack on the Dutch East Indies. To put off such an attack, the common strategy of the companies and the U.S. government was to provide Japan with enough oil to keep the country from feeling cornered—but not with so much oil as to allow the military to build up its stockpiles. Some sources attribute the timing of the Japanese attack on Pearl Harbor and the Dutch East Indies in 1941 to the failure of the U.S. government faithfully to execute its chosen strategy.[33]

In any event, Japan's experiences after seizing the oil fields and refineries of Sumatra and Singapore simply confirmed once again the dangers of having to rely upon foreign-owned sources of crude oil and foreign-owned oil refineries. The careful demolition plans of the foreigners actually had worked in many key installations. Japan was a full year in bringing the Sumatran fields up to 60 percent of their prewar production levels, and the related refineries up to 40 percent of their prewar levels. Even that achievement is said to have required close to 70 percent of the trained personnel available in Japan.[34]

The occupation years that followed the war had various profound effects on the Japanese, contributing to the guardian-ward relationship with the United States. One consequence of that relationship was to temporarily alleviate the anxiety of the Japanese over the security of their access to crude oil. Instead, for about a decade, the country's policy makers turned their minds to methods for securing crude oil at the lowest possible price.[35]

Japan's decision to concentrate on procuring its energy cheaply was altogether consistent with U.S. preferences at the time. During the occupation, the personnel on the Supreme Commander's staff who were responsible for policy toward Japan's oil industry included a number of individuals borrowed from the U.S.-based international oil companies.[36] Their preference, inevitably, was to have the Japanese return to the prewar situation in which foreign firms provided the crude oil and dominated the refining and distribution system of Japan. In the short run, that arrangement also appeared to the Japanese government to be the least costly way by which the country could obtain its needed supplies of crude oil.

The pattern that emerged proved only a shade more complicated. The enterprises of the prewar era did return, joined by one or two newcomers. At the same time, however, the Japanese firms that had gained a foothold in the refining and distribution of petroleum and its products during the war went back into business as well. The upshot was a series of joint ventures. Between 1949 and 1952, using their access to world oil as their principal bargaining counter, Stanvac, Caltex, Union Oil, Shell, and one or two others reentered the Japanese market as the partners of domestic oil firms. By the middle of the decade, the foreign firms and their Japanese partners dominated Japan's oil market.[37] Once again the oil industry was reestablished in Japan as the exceptional case — as the major industry in which foreign interests were dominant.

Shaking off foreign domination. Throughout the 1950s, Japanese policy makers pushed aside various proposals to reduce the degree of foreign domination over the country's domestic oil refining and oil distribution industries, concentrating instead on the acquisition of cheap energy sources.

In the early part of that period, the effort to throw off foreign domination was hobbled in any case by the fact that the Japanese government was determined to rebuild a refinery industry and badly lacked the capital to perform the job. For Japan, the need for refineries was abnormally large because of the country's general policies with respect to the processing of industrial raw materials. There was a determination in all fields to avoid the importation of processed products and to limit imports to materials in their unprocessed state. This meant that a huge refinery industry had to be put in place — a need that seemingly offered foreign firms an opportunity to acquire even greater control of the Japanese petroleum industry.

Although Japan's policy makers were prepared, for the time being, to treat the oil industry as an exceptional case that justified maintaining a high degree of foreign ownership, they could not allow the foreign oil companies to take over the industry altogether. Some degree of independence was being urged by respected national leaders who had been identified with Japan's prewar oil industry.[38] Accordingly, MITI took some measures to hold down the acquisition of new equity by foreigners. Moreover, MITI used its allocation powers to reduce the majors' share of the Japanese market,[39] and it supported one or two projects to develop Japanese oil sources outside the control of the majors.[40] But these were minor achievements, exceptions to its general policy during the 1950s of relying on the foreign-owned international oil companies to supply Japan's oil.

It was not very long, however, before some of the drawbacks of such a policy became apparent. During the 1950s, MITI found itself approving a series of deals between refinery companies that were partly or wholly owned by Japanese interests and individual foreign-owned (mainly U.S.-owned) crude oil suppliers, entailing loans tied to crude oil purchase commitments. Between 1951 and 1961, in fact, twenty-one such loans involving $139 million were authorized, involving nine Japanese borrowers and eight foreign lender-suppliers.[41]

From the viewpoint of achieving an independent Japanese industry, loans were better than equity, particularly as their terms were commonly limited to the five-to-ten-year range. But tying Japan's economy to specified foreign-owned sources had inhibiting consequences for Japan's ability to manage its affairs. For better or worse, this fixed the sources to which Japan could turn in periods of shortage. And it reduced Japan's capacity to shop for bargains in periods of surplus. The inhibitions on Japan's capacity to shop proved especially important in the latter 1950s and early 1960s. Apart from some brief periods of trauma such as the closing of the Suez Canal in 1956, these were years of easy oil supply, in which spot bargains were not uncommon. With tied purchases reaching 80 percent of Japan's oil imports by 1962,[42] the problem began to take on serious proportions in the eyes of the Japanese government.

Nevertheless, larger developments in the world oil markets were beginning to create the conditions by which Japan could recapture control of its domestic industry. By 1962, despite the obstacles, Japan had managed to establish a fairly substantial group of Japanese refiners that were free of equity ties to the majors. Indeed, four such companies — Idemitsu, Maruzen, Daikyo, and Nihon Kogyo — had come to account for nearly 45 percent of Japan's total refining capacity.[43] At the same time, new sources were offering their crude oil to Japanese refiners. The international oil cartel, dominated by six leading firms from 1928 on, had been dissolved in 1948, freeing Gulf, Shell, and Compagnie Française de Pétroles to bid for some of the Japanese market. Moreover, during the 1950s, half a dozen new international firms — most of them American in origin — had developed independent sources of crude oil from North Africa and the Middle East; relative newcomers, such as Union Oil, Standard Oil Company of Indiana, and the American Independent Oil Company (a consortium of ten so-called independent U.S. oil companies), were offering crude oil for sale in Japan.

In 1961, therefore, the Japanese government in effect served notice on the foreign-owned oil companies that it intended to develop new tools to guide the growth of the Japanese market. At that stage, Japan began to repeat its regulatory history of the 1930s. A Petroleum Industry Law was passed in 1962 that assigned to MITI a permanent supervisory role over the development of the industry, including the licensing of refineries, the approval of financial arrangements, the approval of production plans and crude oil acquisition plans, and so on. With new powers of this sort, MITI hoped to be able to reduce Japan's tied oil sales from 80 percent of its purchases to 30 percent.[44]

Looking back at this period, these various steps could easily be interpreted by foreigners as confirmation of the existence of a Japan Incorporated juggernaut, which enlisted the unquestioned support of all sectors of the Japanese economy and proceeded singlemindedly to overcome the foreigners. In fact, each such step encountered plenty of domestic opposition. During the 1950s, individual Japanese firms constantly jockeyed for position in the domestic market, using the resources of their respective foreign partners whenever they could be used to advantage. When MITI first proposed its Petroleum Industry Law in 1961, both the electric power and the steel industry expressed opposition. The ease with which the law was eventually passed is explained in part by the fact that such an open-ended grant of authority for the regulation of an industry was in no way offensive to the fundamental ideology of the country — indeed, was wholly in harmony with the ideology. Despite some selective opposition, the law easily garnered the support of small business organizations, the Petroleum Producers' Association, and the small cluster of special oil companies that were already assuming the role of Japan's national champions in the development of an independent oil industry.[45]

The willingness of industry to countenance a delegation of power to government depended in part, of course, on its expectation that it would have a hand in the exercise of that power. In the case of Japan, there were strong reasons for the expectation. To begin with, the industry's trade association, the Petroleum Association of Japan, was accustomed to acting as MITI's implementing arm, carrying out MITI's production regulation plans under the general guidelines laid down by the ministry. But the strong test of Japanese practice was provided by MITI's handling of disputes with the oil companies.

The importance of national style in the handling of disagreements between government and industry was illustrated in numerous ways. In the first place, the 1962 act contained no overt sanctions of a powerful sort — a fact that led the U.S.-based *Oil and Gas Journal* to assume erroneously that the bill might prove unimportant.[46] After the law's adoption, when a bitter dispute arose between Idemitsu and MITI, fundamentally threatening to the existence of the control system, it took six months of elaborate negotiation to bring Idemitsu back into the fold, during which each side occasionally lost its temper. But by and large, the language of battle was one that emphasized persuasion, cooperation, and the national welfare, and the outcome was one that involved concessions on both sides.[47]

With the adoption of the 1962 petroleum act, the process that would eventually bring a considerable part of Japan's petroleum industry back under the control of Japanese nationals was fairly well launched. Subsequent developments, however, could be attributed only partly to the existence of the appropriate law; more important was the declining power during the 1960s of the guardian-ward relationship between Japan and the United States. By 1967 a Comprehensive Energy Advisory Committee — a typical consensus-building committee of prestigious leaders — was calling for the promotion of independent sources of oil for Japan.[48] But a critical link still had to be created if the Japanese strategy was to work, this link being a direct tie between Japan's refineries and its crude oil sources.

Securing crude oil. Although a considerable proportion of Japan's refinery industry was under the control of Japanese nationals by the early 1970s, nearly 80 percent of the country's crude oil imports still went through the vertical channels of the big multinational oil companies. Most of that total went to supply the refineries and distribution networks in which these foreign companies had an equity interest; the rest went to nationally owned entities. MITI therefore was still far from the national objective of controlling some of the channels by which the country imported its crude oil.

To that end, well before the 1973 embargo, MITI was already encouraging a number of different initiatives. In 1967 the Petroleum Development Corporation was created, charged with subsidizing some of the overseas exploration activities of Japanese firms and with assisting in the financing of their development activities. By 1973 the corporation was expending a little more than $100 million on loans and investments. Between 1969 and 1973 the Mitsui, Mitsubishi, and Sumitomo groups each created their own petroleum development corporations as vehicles for promoting the groups' overseas activities in crude oil and petroleum refining. In the same period, the trading firms of C. Itoh and Marubeni undertook major initiatives of a similar sort. The results were apparent in the rapid growth of Japan's overseas exploration. Between 1968 and 1973 the number of Japanese firms engaged in such exploration rose from 8 to 49, the number of wells drilled rose from 44 to 180, and expenditures on exploration and development rose from $44 million to $488 million.

Although Japan fared comparatively well at the hands of the majors during the 1973 oil embargo,[49] the episode accelerated Japan's search for independent sources of crude oil. Japan's new efforts were based upon the assumption that the guardian-ward relation was ended — that in a pinch the country would get no help from the United States or from other industrialized countries with which Japan was associated through the Organization for Economic Cooperation and Development.[50] An agreement among most of the OECD countries to share their oil resources in a period of scarcity, it was assumed, would be ineffectual in an emergency. With Japan's pervasive sense of isolation and deprivation, it was not surprising that this should be the country's basic planning assumption.

To get its new approach off the ground, the government in 1974 followed its customary pratice of mobilizing all sectors of the economy to the new public objective. MITI formed an Advisory Committee for Energy, which was charged to develop a series of national goals. In the years subsequent, that body and others repeatedly proposed quantitative goals and the policies by which they might be reached.[51]

Meanwhile, the government pressed ahead with new efforts to secure its own sources of foreign oil. In October 1973, 120 Japanese companies from assorted industries created a Japan Cooperation Center for the Middle East, intended to lubricate the communication process with the area. In 1974 those efforts blossomed into a full-fledged plan that would engage oil-producing countries in "cooperative economic resource diplomacy." The program envisaged several interrelated elements, most of which could be found to some extent in the national programs of other governments: government-to-government agreements would provide a long-term framework for the conduct of large-scale investment and trading activities; individual Japanese firms, operating in partnership with one another and with the government-owned enterprises, would provide technology and capital for development projects; and refineries in Japan would provide the markets for the exporters' crude oil.

The Japanese plans differed from those of most other governments, however, in one critical respect: despite bitter squabbling among its various national interests, and despite charges of incompetence and rigidity on the part of the Japanese bureaucracy, Japan succeeded in implementing its plans to a degree that other governments found difficult to achieve.[52] Once the formal plan was adopted, Japan set about expanding its loans to the area through various channels, including the country's Export-Import Bank and its Overseas Economic Cooperation Fund. By the end of 1976, Japan had signed economic and technical cooperation agreements with Iraq, Saudi Arabia, Iran, and Qatar.

In terms of the immediate objective of securing independent sources of crude oil, results were a little slow in coming. By 1978 crude oil imports arranged through governments or by direct deals between Japanese importers and state exporters came to only 19.4 percent of Japan's total crude oil imports. Even that limited performance depended largely on Iraq's stepped up exports, which were linked to a $1 billion loan by Japan to that country. When added to other crude oil imports arranged outside the networks of the multinational oil companies, these supplies did little to improve Japan's position of independence.

But the Japanese government persisted. And in 1978, when Iran's revolution and its war with Iraq again created an international oil crisis, its efforts were intensified. By 1980 it was evident that Japan's long-run program for freeing itself from multinational sources was beginning to bear fruit. By that time, Iran, Abu Dhabi, Qatar, Saudi Arabia, and Kuwait had been added to the list of Japan's heavy suppliers, and direct deals of various sorts were generating 45 percent of Japan's crude oil imports.[53] By that year, too, the supplies provided by the multinational enterprises had been cut back to about 45 percent of Japan's crude oil requirements.

If there were unique elements in Japan's program for the acquisition of independent sources of crude oil, however, they were associated with the way in which the partnerships, consortia, and trading companies of the country performed to implement the national campaign. Consortia of this sort drew their strength from various features: their direct sponsorship by the Japanese government as chosen instruments for the execution of government-to-government deals; their direct linkage, through some of their participants, to official sources of equity investment, credit, and guarantees; and a capacity, especially through the big trading houses, to accept payment in the form of commodities, as well as a capacity to offer a wide range of technical services and capital equipment in integrated deals. In Saudi Arabia, for instance, this set of capabilities was evident in two such groups, both headed by Mitsubishi; by 1980 one group had brought eleven years of planning to a successful close with a commitment for a 450,000-ton ethylene plant, while the other had undertaken to build and operate a 730,000-ton methanol plant.[54]

Despite these efforts at diversification and linkage, Japan's economy still seemed to face considerable uncertainties in the early 1980s. With very few vertical links back to their sources of crude oil supply, the Japanese refiners and distributors faced high financial risks. Their import costs were being determined by two prices, both disconcertingly volatile: the dollar price for oil demanded by the exporters, and the dollar-yen exchange rate. Sometimes the two rates worked in opposite directions, stabilizing their costs; at other times the two rates moved in a common direction, exposing the industry to large losses.[55] Questions of security obviously remained much on the minds of Japanese officials and businessmen. But at least the country had achieved its first objective — that of getting some of the tools of oil policy out of the control of foreigners and back into its own hands.

The Basic Metals

In the basic metals, during the three or four decades following the end of World War II, the Japanese economy managed to get even closer to achieving a national sense of security of supply, despite the economy's heavy reliance on foreign sources. Some profound changes in the supply structure of the metallic ores were critical in helping the Japanese move so swiftly toward their goal.

Developing supplies. At the beginning of the period the dependent situation of Japan was almost as pronounced in the case of metallic ores as it had been in oil. The option of developing some domestic sources of supply for metallic ores existed in Japan only with respect to copper, lead, and zinc. And as Japan's economy mushroomed and its needs grew, such sources were obviously too limited to supply any substantial part of the country's needs.

The metal industries differed from oil, however, in one important respect: their domestic processing facilities were always owned by Japanese interests. Accordingly, the country's strategy could be much more straightforward. From the first, MITI's objective was to develop secure foreign sources for the unprocessed ores while building up the home processing industry. In the 1950s, immediately following the end of the military occupation, the problems presented for the Japanese economy by the principal metals industries were part of a much larger problem — that of an inadequate supply of foreign exchange. Within the limits imposed by foreign exchange availabilities, the Japanese bought their foreign requirements largely on the spot market. In the decades that followed, the swift growth of their economy and the gradual depletion of their limited domestic sources of ore required the Japanese to launch a much more aggressive approach for developing foreign sources of raw materials.

In 1963 MITI established a subsidiary, the Metal Mining Agency of Japan. In the first few years of its life, the agency concentrated on domestic exploration, mainly of copper and lead, paying out a steady stream of subsidies on a modest scale — on the order of 3 billion yen annually.[56] By 1968, however, the agency was promoting loans for exploration and development in foreign locations, and by 1973 these expenditures were being made at a rate of 2 billion yen annually.[57] That support was used as seed money to help foreign mine operators develop new sources of supply for Japanese markets. Japan's willingness — indeed, in many cases, its eagerness — to enter into long-term contracts for the output of the mines gave the mine owners an improved basis for borrowing in international markets. Lending banks in Europe and the United States could comfort themselves with the hope that in times of glut Japanese buyers would favor the sources with which they held such contracts.[58]

An additional element in Japan's strategy was to organize its principal users of metal ores into buying groups, with a designated leader who conducted the negotiations for the group in any given country; Nippon Steel, for instance, handled all of the Japanese steel industry's major iron ore and coal purchases in Australia. The power of such buying groups was considerable from the first, inasmuch as many of the exporting countries found themselves relying on the Japanese market as their principal buyers. By the latter 1970s, Australia was selling over three-quarters of its exports of both iron ore and copper ore to Japan. India, too, was exporting about three-quarters of its iron ore exports to Japan, while Brazil was relying upon the Japanese market for the sale of one-third of its exports of ore.[59] These buying strategies were reinforced by Japan's tariff policies, which closely paralleled those traditionally used by the United States. Whereas ores were typically admitted without duty, processed metals usually bore significant duties[60]

A very early version of Japan's policies could be seen in the case of copper, a product in which the perils of instability seemed especially marked for Japan. Japanese firms were obliged to buy their foreign copper ore on the basis of prices that were greatly influenced by the copper quotations of the London Metals Exchange, quotations that were notoriously unstable. It was probably no coincidence, therefore, that the Japanese government allowed its copper-refining firms to make investments in foreign copper mines earlier and on a larger scale than was the case for other metal-processing industries. As early as 1953, for instance, when Japan was in a difficult balance-of-payments situation, it was already providing financial assistance to a copper mine in the Philippines.[61] In subsequent years, Japan extended loans and guarantees to copper mines in Canada, Papua New Guinea, Indonesia, and Malaysia.[62] By the latter 1960s, the Japanese were not only lending to foreign copper mines but also taking equity interests in such mines, including operations in Zaire, Malaysia, Canada, Peru, and Chile.[63] By 1973 the nation's Overseas Development Guarantee Fund had reached about $95 million.

It was evident by the mid-1970s that Japan was making the most of the fortuitous discoveries of vast quantities of ores in Australia. The payoff was enlarged not only by Japan's practice of pooling its national buying through a single agent but also by the country's systematic efforts to reduce shipping costs. As a matter of national policy, Japan took the lead in developing large ore-carrying ships. In 1953 Japan had no ore vessels that exceeded 20,000 tons. But by the 1970s Japan had acquired 150 such vessels, with a total ore-carrying capacity of over 5.6 million tons; and by 1980 it had 206 such vessels, with a capacity of 10.2 million tons.[64] The consequence was a sharp reduction in the cost of Japan's ocean freight.[65]

By almost any measure, the performance of Japanese industry in securing its ores during the 1960s could be counted as an extraordinary success. It was helped, to be sure, by a great stroke of luck—the fact that nearby Australia was so rich in the needed resources. But Japanese policies seemed to be making the most of the god-given opportunities.

The uncertainties of long-term contracts. By the end of the 1960s, Japanese imports of metallic ores rested mainly on the efficacy of long-term loans or other long-term financial assistance from the government, coupled with long-term contracts and coordinated national buying.[66] Despite the seeming success of Japan's policies during the 1960s, however, the Japanese may have thought of themselves as pursuing a second-best strategy in this period. This was a time in which American firms — and European ones only a little less so — were relying heavily on vertical integration for the security of their foreign supplies of bauxite, copper ore, and iron ore.

Of course, in the 1960s Japan would have had great difficulty in pursuing a strategy of actual ownership on a broad scale. Some Japanese investors were being allowed to take small equity positions in foreign copper mines. But generalizing that policy to all important minerals would have required vast quantities of capital. Besides, it would have placed latecomer Japanese firms in direct competition with well established U.S. and European firms for mining concessions in third countries, a competition that the Japanese were not yet prepared to face. Finally, Japan would have had to overcome the latent or active hostility of many developing countries to any foreign investments in raw materials, a hostility that would come to a head in the early 1970s in a great rash of nationalizations. Long-term investments of a less massive and less intrusive sort may have been seen as a safer course for trying to reduce the uncertainties of supply.

But the policy of relying solely on long-term contracts seemed to entail high risks. The first Australian call for renegotiation of long-term iron ore contracts came in 1966, before the ink on the contracts had dried, and it became clear very early that such contracts would not be providing the degree of stability of supply and price that Japan constantly sought.[67] The various Australian states showed little disposition or ability to pool their bargaining power effectively.[68] But threatening noises in that direction were sufficiently frequent to keep the Japanese on edge.

In the 1970s, therefore, the Japanese responded to the obvious instability of their situation by increasing their equity holdings in overseas mines. Having already invested extensively in copper mines, they began to move at this stage into other types of ore. In iron ore, such equity investments appeared in Brazil, Peru, and Australia; by 1980 Japanese interests held equity in four of Australia's eight mammoth iron ore mines.[69] And in aluminum, Japan acquired equity interests in a string of smelters and bauxite mines spread throughout New Zealand, Venezuela, Canada, Indonesia, Brazil, Australia, and the United States.[70] These investments rarely entailed actual management commitments on the part of the Japanese, but they did entail a less transitory involvement.

Apart from increasing Japan's right to call on the output of specified mines, Japan's increased emphasis on equity investment also had another purpose. As the fragility of long-term contracts grew evident, banks proved less willing to finance new mines on the basis of such contracts alone. Equity investment thus came to substitute for the banking role that long-term contracts had served in the past. It was widely assumed in financial circles that in times of glut the Japanese would treat mines in which they held some equity more favorably than other mines, thereby reducing the lending risk; and there is some evidence that the assumption was justified.[71]

By the early 1980s, the Japanese practice of taking equity interests in overseas mining facilities had been well established. As a rule the size of the interest was not much over 10 percent. But by that time, about half of the country's supplies of iron ore were coming from foreign mines in which Japanese had an equity interest, and similar tendencies were visible in the other ores. How far Japan would go in that direction in an effort to bolster its sense of security was not yet clear.

The country's efforts to improve its access to foreign sources of ore and metal extended also to some of the policies it was following at home. The stockpile policy of the Japanese government, undertaken in earnest in the 1970s, was a logical extension of its policy of trying to increase its security of supplies through long-term contracts. The drawback of such contracts is that they usually commit the buyer over a long period of time to some minimum quantity of purchases, irrespective of the buyer's needs. That restraint had embarrassed Japanese metal-ore buyers during the 1960s and 1970s, whenever demand temporarily fell. In response to that problem, it appears that in the early 1970s the steel companies had already created a stockpile whose function was to take up their surplus steel production. Finally, in 1976, the Japanese government helped set up a number of such stockpiles, by lending funds to the stockpile associations at preferential credit rates.

Here again, the difference between Japan's policies and those of the United States are worth noting. In the U.S. case, stockpiles for various metals and ores had been created in the 1940s ostensibly in response to a strategic need, not as an economic device for the stabilization of markets; justifying their existence by viewing them as stabilizing devices would have been offensive to American ideology. Nevertheless, without a coherent long-term policy, the American stockpiles were used from time to time as stabilizing devices, in response to short-term pressures that built up in the U.S. economy. In contrast, the Japanese government, unencumbered by ideological considerations to the contrary, maintained its stockpiles explicitly for stabilizing purposes.[72] Accordingly, having acquired about 72,000 metric tons of copper in 1976 and 1977, the government fed out 64,000 tons from 1978 to 1980; and having acquired 22,000 tons of aluminum from 1976 to 1978, it sold its holdings in 1979, only to buy again heavily in 1981.[73]

Transactions of this sort eased the burden of Japanese processors in fulfilling their long-term commitments to buy foreign ores. But they also served another important purpose. During the 1970s it became clear that Japan's handicaps as a result of the high cost of energy and the limited availability of space for industry would present formidable difficulties for Japanese metal-processing industries. Besides, some developing countries with which Japan was eager for firmer economic relations had the energy, the space, and the capital to expand those very industries. The government, therefore, set about trying to persuade Japanese firms in some of these industries that their future in Japan was insecure. By 1974 this perception was being built into the agreed-upon views of government and industry, and was being reflected in MITI projections of the economy. And by the early 1980s specific plans were on the way to implementation.

The decline of uncertainty. By the early 1980s, Japan could look back on several decades of remarkable success in the procurement of its basic needs for key industrial materials. With good luck and careful planning, the country had managed to acquire its needed materials on adequate terms. Indeed, in iron ore and bauxite it had managed to better its terms over the years by comparison with those available to U.S. importers, and in copper ores it had managed to keep abreast of the United States (see Figures 5.1, 5.2, and 5.3). With such a record, the

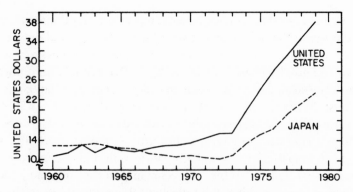

Figure 5.1. Price of iron ore used in steelmaking, c.i.f. price per metric ton, 1960–1979.

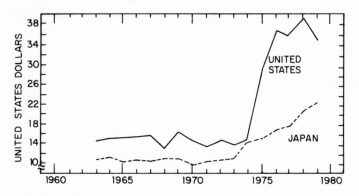

Figure 5.2. Price of bauxite, c.i.f. price per metric ton. 1960–1979.

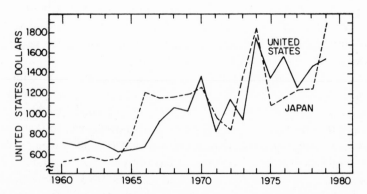

Figure 5.3. Price of copper ores and concentrates, c.i.f. price per metric ton of copper content, 1960–1979.

country's confidence in its ability to procure critically needed products from abroad could not fail to grow.

The apparent growth in Japan's confidence with respect to its mineral supplies appears to be part of a broader change in the country's perception of itself as a have-not nation. This critical shift is suggested by Japan's plans for adjusting to the high cost of energy. The 1970s had impressed two critical facts on Japanese policy makers: first, that the country's scarce land and acute environmental needs limited the extent to which industries such as metal processing could be placed on Japanese territory; and, second, that Japan ran the risk of being a high-cost user of energy. Confronting these factors, Japan has resolutely determined to shrink some of its energy-using industries.

Japan's plans to cut back its aluminum industry in an effort to reduce its uses of high-cost energy represent a particularly striking manifestation of the country's increased confidence in its capacity to procure key materials from abroad.[74] The demand for aluminum in Japan is expected to grow rapidly during the 1980s. But according to MITI's plans, all of the increase will be supplied from foreign production. On the other hand, Japan has no intention of leaving its needs to the

---

Sources: FIGURE 5.1: Robert W. Crandall, *The U.S. Steel Industry in Recurrent Crisis* (Washington, D.C.: Brookings Institution, 1981), p. 21; 1977–79 figures from United Nations, *World Trade Annual 1977, 1978, and 1979*, vol. 1 (New York: Walker and Company, 1979, 1980, and 1981); U.S. 1977–79 figures adjusted by the freight index in World Bank, *Commodity Trade and Price Trends* (Baltimore: Johns Hopkins University Press, 1980), p. 34. FIGURE 5.2: For the United States: Leonard L. Fischman, project director, *World Mineral Trends and U.S. Supply Problems*, Research Paper R-20 (Washington, D.C.: Resources for the Future, 1980), p. 370. For Japan: United Nations, *World Trade Annual*, vol. 1 (New York, 1966–1980); idem, *Yearbook of International Trade Statistics* (New York, 1960–1965). FIGURE 5.3: For the United States: Fischman, *World Mineral Trends*, p. 392, adjusted by rates on pp. 394–395 to arrive at c.i.f. figures; Metal Bulletin, *Metal Bulletin Handbook* (Surrey, England, 1981). For Japan: United Nations, *World Trade Annual*, vol. 1 (New York, 1966–1980); idem, *Yearbook of International Trade Statistics* (New York, 1960–1965); Mia de Kuijper, "The International Copper Industry," Program on U.S.-Japan Relations, Center for International Affairs, Harvard University, May 1981, appendix VI.18; W. Gluschke et al., *Copper: The Next Fifteen Years* (Dordrecht, Holland: D. Reidel, 1979), pp. 156–157.

Note: C.i.f. = cost, insurance, and freight included in price.

vagaries of the international market: the largest part is to come from the carefully diversified sources in which Japan has accumulated its equity interests.

The Japanese approach to the petroleum-refining industry was still being formulated in 1982, but it also appeared to involve a freeze on the growth of that industry in Japan.[75] At the same time, the Japanese were encouraging their petrochemicals producers to develop joint ventures with producers in other countries, in a pattern described as "horizontal specialization." The pattern implied a certain amount of cross-hauling of products between affiliates, suggesting once again that Japan was prepared to accept some of the risks of relying on foreign sources for part of its vital supplies.[76] In the same spirit, Japan has even been showing signs of a willingness to rely on foreign sources for a minuscule portion of its steel supplies. A few of Japan's complex deals for importing Brazilian iron ore, for instance, have entailed importing steel as well.[77]

In light of Japan's long history of concern over its basic materials, its decision to rely upon some importation of these vital supplies is quite extraordinary. It suggests that Japan is at last capable of confronting its import vulnerabilities with a certain equanimity. That equanimity is not based, however, on serendipity, but rests on a strategy that calls for the diversification of sources and the use of long-term organic ties to suppliers. Rational responses of that sort can be expected to continue in the future.

6

FEEDING
THE
GIANTS

The dominant position of Japan and the United States in the world markets for oil and hard minerals suggests that in a decade or two there will be many points of contact, thereby raising the possibilities of conflict or collaboration. But there is another possibility as well — namely, that their dominant positions may evaporate, reducing the likelihood of extensive interaction. The first task of the seer, therefore, is to explore the likely future developments of these markets, looking especially for clues to the position of these two countries and the nature of their problems.

Through a Glass Darkly

The oil projections. When projecting the future relations of Japan and the United States in acquiring supplies of oil, the central question for the crystal ball is whether shortages will prevail or whether the market will be in easy supply. Because so many critical political issues turn on that question, the past ten years have provided a field day for those who enjoy projecting future developments in the oil market. Large-scale formal models have been especially in demand. These have been produced under the auspices of various international oil companies, the Organization for Economic Cooperation and Development, Japan's Ministry of International Trade and Industry, the International Institute for Applied Systems Analysis, and scores of other sponsoring sources. The 1970s, however, were an especially difficult period for modeling the oil market. Analysts were obliged to work in unknown territory, guessing about relationships that had never previously been experienced.

The question of demand has been especially baffling. In 1973, when the price of oil rose to over $10 a barrel for the first time, there was no previous experience on which modelers could rely. They could guess — and most guessed rightly — that a doubling of prices would produce only a 10 or 15 percent decline in the consumption of oil; but that guess was good only for as long as industrial plants had not yet modified their production processes or altered their structures, and for as long as consumers had not yet traded in their automobiles or insulated their homes. Eventually, as these changes began to take hold, higher demand elasticities began to appear and consumption began to fall. How far that process would eventually affect energy consumption remains a question mark even today.

Understanding how the demand for oil varies is especially critical for the 1980s and 1990s because it has now become apparent that the price of oil is not immune to periods of decline. As energy users come to realize this, it is not clear how consumption levels will be affected. Will the trend to conservation be reversed? Or will the uncertainties of the future be sufficient to continue the conservation momentum for a period of time?

Projecting the supply of oil during the parlous period since 1973 has been even more difficult than projecting demand. To begin with, there is the inscrutable role played by the Soviet Union. Although the Soviet Union was a net exporter of oil during the early 1970s in the amount of several million barrels a day, mainly to its Comecon partners in Eastern Europe, its future behavior is understandably obscure. Informed guesses at various times have ranged from an expectation that the Soviet Union would continue its existing level of exports to an expectation that by the 1980s it would switch to being a large net importer.

Outside the Soviet Union, there has been another question just as difficult to answer: How many new discoveries would be induced by the extraordinary price levels that were beginning to appear? The self-assured assertions of some oil geologists in the early 1970s that all major deposits were already known have proved to be misleading. The expanded production of oil and gas in Mexico, the altered prospects for gas production in the Soviet Union, the added production extracted from existing U.S. oil fields, and the numerous discoveries of oil and gas in smaller quantities elsewhere have changed the supply picture considerably, contributing to the decline in the importance of OPEC sources. For the modelers, all these sources of supply were unmapped territory, entailing errors of estimate that could easily run to many million barrels a day by the 1980s. As events turned out, such errors proved common.

Perhaps the greatest uncertainty of all has centered on the pricing and production decisions of the oil-exporting countries. Those charged with building formal models usually made the assumption that the OPEC countries would exercise their quasi-monopolistic powers to the fullest, coordinating their pricing and production decisions to extract the highest possible collective return. A few aberrant economists, sizing up the prospects soon after the oil crisis of 1973, were of a very different mind, being persuaded that in spite of OPEC a collapse in the world price of oil was quite imminent, after which some form of workable competition would set in.[1]

Reality proved more complex than either assumption. What followed could be described as the behavior of a weak oligopoly, operating in markets with very low elasticities and including participants with widely different views of what the oligopoly ought to achieve. Some participants favored economic maximizing in the short run, some in the long run. Some had their eye on one political objective, some on another.

In the end, the thirteen disparate countries that have made up OPEC's membership have proved too many and too diverse in position and interest to maintain an effective set of agreements, especially in an array of markets as complex as those for crude oil and its products. From time to time, OPEC members formally agreed on new price levels for their oil, and for a little while in 1982 they were even formally agreed on production ceilings. But with so many member states operating in so many markets with so many products, it was always difficult for any of the members to know if others were adhering fully to the price agreements. Planned cutbacks in production did occur on occasion, sometimes as a result of the considered decisions of the OPEC countries — notably of Saudi Arabia, operating to serve its complex national goals. But more typically the observed cutbacks seemed due to the fact that the marketing channels disposing of the national output seemed unable in the short run to sell the current production.

Confronting a formidable array of imponderables on both the supply side and the demand side of the oil market in the early 1970s, any analyst could rationally have been pushed to the conclusion that the range of plausible projections over a five- or ten-year period was extraordinarily wide. Only a few tendencies seemed reasonably clear. The analyst could assume, for instance, that world production and world consumption would grow steadily over the long run. And it would not be utterly reckless to assume that some of the older, well exploited sources of production, including notably the United States, would face stagnant or declining production trends. Beyond such generalizations, however, the possibilities covered so wide a range as easily to encompass both shortage and glut. Small annual changes in supply and demand elasticities, small differences in the projected role of the Soviet Union, and small variations in the behavior of OPEC or the fortunes of the oil explorers or the speed of technological change could produce widely disparate outcomes.

Model builders, however, are not ordinarily allowed the luxury of projecting a range of outcomes, especially when the range encompasses the possibility of both shortage and glut.[2] Policy makers and opinion formers commonly insist on the illusion of certainty, even when that option is not realistically available.[3] As a result, the typical projections of the mid-1970s foresaw a sustained period of oil shortages; and as the years went on, the projections were progressively modified until by the early 1980s they were commonly pointing to the possibility of some years of glut.[4]

Today, the policy maker is still confronted with the need to project. But the uncertainties of the 1970s have not abated, and the likely outcomes cover as wide a range as ever.

The minerals projections. The problems associated with modeling the future of the mineral markets have not been much easier than those associated with oil. Indeed, in one important respect the mineral markets have offered even greater difficulties for projection. The market for any mineral is extremely sensitive to the changes in the metal industry on which it depends. But the metal industries are typically composed of relatively few users organized in oligopolistic arrangements. The future behavior of users of this sort is especially difficult to specify.

Not surprisingly, therefore, the range of possibilities that plausible models of the mineral industries have produced has been as wide as the range in petroleum, encompassing the possibility of both glut and shortage. Guesses about the future demand for the metals on which the mineral markets depend have been difficult. For instance, departing from the usual official pattern of providing point estimates, the U.S. Department of the Interior places the U.S. demand for aluminum in the year 2000 at 10–26 million short tons, and the demand for copper at 3.5–6 million tons.[5] (For reasons that are unclear, the projections for iron ore cover an implausibly narrow range, running at 108–132 million tons.)[6]

Apart from the problems of projecting the demand for the various minerals, there is also the problem of projecting the market structure in which they will be sold.   In varying degrees, the structure of the mineral markets went through major changes in the 1960s and 1970s. Australia emerged as a cornucopia for iron ore and bauxite; Brazil became a gargantuan supplier of iron ore with aspirations to enter the bauxite and aluminum markets on a large scale; the United States reemerged as a huge exporter of coal.

At the same time, in practically all products, changes in market structure presaged greater price volatility and greater uncertainty for users of the metals and of the ores required for their fabrication. A considerable portion of the costs of production in these products is fixed, especially for firms that are not in a position to reduce their labor force in a period of decline; the demand and supply elasticities in the short run remain quite low; and the adjustments suggested by changes in market price are a long time in coming. Moreover, the changes in the structure of the oil and metals industries add to the risks of instability. In copper, the possibilities for stabilizing action on the part of a private oligopoly have almost disappeared, while the links between the metal producers and the metal fabricators have been greatly weakened. In aluminum, the oligopoly has persisted, albeit weakened by an increase in the number of firms and by the fact that a few state-owned enterprises have moved into the marketing of bauxite and alumina. In iron ore, the sedate long-term supplier arrangements of the industry have been upset by the nationalization of foreign-owned mines in a few countries and by the persistent fragility of long-term contractual commitments on prices and quantities.

At the same time that the stability which once came from vertical integration and tacit oligopolistic agreements has declined, the increased predictability that might have taken its place through a regime of workable competition has not appeared. Although the number of producers has increased in most metal markets, it would be rash to assume that the increase in numbers offers any early promise of more efficient markets. As we observed earlier, state-owned enterprises in the mining business have special difficulties in responding to the signals of the market, especially if the response entails cutting back on production.

The uncertainties of the 1970s, therefore, are being replaced by a new set of uncertainties in the 1980s. On the demand side, the confusing signals offered by volatile prices in copper, and perhaps even in iron ore and bauxite, may profoundly alter the uses of these materials in the long term. Many industrial users of raw materials see stability in the price of inputs as a major virtue. Industrial users whose own output confronts a low price elasticity of demand are sometimes more interested in stable prices for their raw materials than in low ones. Accordingly, some oil users could shift to coal; some steel and copper users to optic fibers, plastics, and ceramics. The common problems that the United States and Japan share in the hard metals, therefore, could easily prove to be those that go with surplus rather than with shortage.[7]

The location of world industry. Apart from changes in the global supply-demand balance in some of these minerals, there is also the possibility of major changes induced by shifts in the location of the user industries. Japan has already shown clear signs of its intention to limit the growth of energy-using industries such as aluminum, petroleum refining, and petrochemicals, by relying on the imports of these products to fill part of its needs. European governments are already acceding, albeit reluctantly, to a decline in their steelmaking capacities.[8] Even the United States, while unwilling to acknowledge explicitly any specific goals in its industrial mix, is under pressure to let its steel industry shrink.[9]

Meanwhile, the plans of the developing countries to expand their industrial facilities over the next few decades are being widely advertised and vigorously pushed. The oil exporters, as we saw in Chapter 2, have ambitious plans for processing their crude oil into products. Countries with ample supplies of gas are already taking steps to install large energy-using industries such as aluminum smelters and steel plants. At the same time, the so-called newly industrialized countries — such as Brazil, India, and Korea — are practically certain to expand their output of products that use up industrial raw materials in quantity. Australia and Canada, too, may use much greater quantities of industrial raw materials than in the past. In many cases, these shifts in production may reduce the volume of industrial raw materials available for export; and in other cases, such as those of India, Mexico, and China, the shifts may place in the market new bidders for the available materials, alongside Japan and the United States. The dominance of the United States and Japan in these markets, so evident in the 1970s, could rapidly diminish so that any discussion of their bilateral relationship would lose some of its relevance.

On the other hand, we may be entering a period in which changes in the structure of world markets will not be as rapid as they were in the past. The slower rates of growth in incomes and outputs that seem to confront the mature industrialized economies of the world could slow down the rate at which new technologies are introduced and new production locations are sought. In the past, Japan has drawn some of its strength and flexibility from the operation of a virtuous circle: its rapid growth has helped the country shift its productive resources to new activities that provided the basis for more growth. For the 1980s, MITI anticipates a much slower growth rate, 4 or 5 percent per annum rather than the 8 or 10 percent that was characteristic in prior decades.[10] A Japanese economy whose growth was reduced to such levels for a sustained period could find itself quite reluctant in the end to restrain or curtail its production of steel, petrochemicals, and aluminum, and could remain a giant consumer of industrial raw materials.

The U.S. economy, too, may continue to place a heavy reliance on imported raw materials. The tendency of the U.S. economy to solve its problems of dependence by stepping up its use of domestic resources of energy and minerals could force it in the end to rely even more heavily on foreign sources of raw materials. The two giants, therefore, may continue to dominate the world's raw material markets.

Oil in a Parlous World

Prudence suggests that the United States and Japan think of the problems they are likely to encounter if their present joint dependence on imported oil continues.

Problems of shortage. In a world awash with uncertainties, the one projection that can be made with a fairly high measure of assurance is that, over the next decade or so, the supply of oil will suffer a sharp interruption, involving some millions of barrels a day. The precise scenario is difficult to predict: civil disturbances in Saudi Arabia or the Persian Gulf emirates, an Iranian air attack on Saudi oil terminals, a threat to free passage in the Straits of Hormuz at the mouth of the Persian Gulf, or a dozen other possibilities affecting the Middle East. On a smaller scale, Indonesia, Libya, Algeria, Mexico, Nigeria, or Venezuela could suffer temporary interruptions in their role as oil exporters. None of these prospective events, taken by itself, carries a high probability; but cumulatively, the likelihood that one or more of them will occur seems high.

For the present, the first line of response of both the United States and Japan to a short interruption of this type consists of the stockpiles held in private and public hands in the two countries. A second line of defense is a sharing arrangement organized under the banner of the International Energy Agency. But the ideological reluctance of the U.S. government to consider how the sharing formula might actually work in an emergency practically guarantees that it will not work very well. Besides, according to the formula that triggers the sharing provision, only an interruption of the first magnitude — such as a total shutdown of Saudi Arabian exports or of several other countries combined — would bring the plan into play. Short of such a contingency, the rule among the oil-importing countries is *suave qui peut*.

To deal with threats of this sort, Japan has been building up its oil stockpiles quite rapidly. By 1981 the oil supplies held in such stockpiles covered slightly over one hundred days of consumption. Although the stockpiles were mostly in private hands, the Japanese government could be expected to have unquestioned control over the supplies in times of emergency. At such times, too, the Japanese government could be expected to scout the world's oil markets for more supplies. It is improbable that Japan would rush into the spot market to acquire the added oil; that approach was tried in 1978 and 1979, with disastrous results. More likely, Japan would use a more comprehensive and less obvious approach, an extension of the practices it had been developing in the 1970s. Such an approach combines purchases of oil with the purchase or sale of nonoil products, long-term loans, and other economic or political undertakings.

The U.S. response to a short-term emergency is likely to be a good deal less effective. To be sure, the United States has been building up its official supplies of oil, albeit more slowly than Japan; by mid-1982 U.S. official supplies amounted to about sixty-five days of prospective imports. In addition to official supplies, there were also privately held supplies that amounted to about ninety-five days of imports. However, private holders of oil stocks in the United States could not be counted on as a buffer in a time of scarcity. And the possibility that the U.S. government would assume control of such stocks appears slight, unless the shortage were quite extreme.

Even as regards U.S. official reserves of oil, it is not at all clear to what extent they may be available in a future crisis. If oil were to be in easy supply for a year or two before the emergency, history suggests that the stockpile itself might begin to melt away. The temptation to balance the federal budget or improve the trade balance by liquidating some of the stockpile could prove too tempting for a harassed administration to resist. Perhaps more important is the disconcerting possibility, repeatedly demonstrated in the history of U.S. regulation, that the merits of releasing official stocks or mobilizing private stocks would become the subject of prolonged public debate.[11]

If a lasting shortage of oil should develop, both Japan and the United States will have to reckon with some new difficulties imposed by the oil-exporting countries. In those circumstances, the past behavior of oil-exporting countries suggests that they would cut back their sales of crude oil to multinational firms, such as those undertaken through Aramco in Saudi Arabia and Petroven in Venezuela, and would expand the direct marketing of the state-owned oil companies. At the same time, the oil exporters would expand their existing plans to manufacture refined oil products and petrochemicals and would force those products on distributors in the importing countries. It will be remembered that Saudi Arabia moved strongly in that direction during the oil shortages of the late 1970s, with its offers of "entitlement oil," doled out to foreign firms that had agreed to help build processing facilities in Saudi Arabia. A return to that kind of policy seems altogether plausible.

Faced with that contingency, Japan would be back to making the best deal it could. It would resign itself to curtailing its refinery and petrochemicals operations in Japan, as it has already shown some inclination to do, and would concentrate its resources on the acquisition of adequate supplies of oil, whether in crude or product form. The United States, on the other hand, would be expected to behave in a rather different manner. As U.S. refineries and petrochemicals plants found themselves pressed by the reduced flow of crude oil and the increased flow of petroleum products, the affected firms would almost certainly demand increased protection from such imports, especially if the products were coming from state-owned exporters with which they had no vertical links. Under the operations of the U.S. law, with its emphasis on the avoidance of dumping and export subsidies, refineries and petrochemical plants would probably be able to secure some degree of protection from foreign imports.[12]

If the United States selected that policy route, the consequences for relations with Japan would show up in the competition of the oil-using industries of the two countries; U.S. industries would be using higher-cost supplies of such products than Japanese industries. Differences of that sort have created trade difficulties in the past, although the differences have usually run in the opposite direction. The ability of U.S. textile firms to acquire relatively cheap oil-based chemical fibers during the late 1970s, for instance, was the subject of a bitter debate with foreign competitors over the possibility of unfair competition. This time, it could be Japan's turn to secure the cheap oil supplies.

In the event of a prolonged oil shortage, however, one has to explore the possibility that the U.S. government might use its exporting capabilities as a bargaining weapon to secure an increased share of the world's supply. Compared with Japan, the capacity of the U.S. economy to mobilize economic muscle seems formidable: in terms of money, technology, food exports, or access to markets, the U.S. economy's weight is unambiguously greater than that of Japan. But the comparison is quite meaningless. Under its existing statutory authority, the U.S. executive branch would have no clear way of linking the country's exports of goods, technology, or money to the acquisition of oil. It would stretch precedent and imagination considerably to picture a situation in which prospective U.S. importers and exporters could be brought together in a common negotiating structure managed by government officials. And if the U.S. executive branch tried to find some way to create an effective structure, the odds are very high that the Congress or the courts would prevent it.

Still, if an oil shortage were sufficiently threatening, the U.S. government might conceivably overcome all the formidable difficulties that stand in the way of mobilizing its negotiating power, and might use preferences and other devices to extract added supplies from oil

exporting countries. Some of the inhibitions that have heretofore restrained the U.S. government from pursuing discriminatory trading
policies on a broad scale have rapidly been weakening, as we saw in
Chapter 1. Although the sentiment for an open world trading system
still runs fairly deep in the United States, the chance that the country
may use selective and discriminatory devices to shape its international
trade patterns is greater than it has been for many decades.

If the U.S. government were eventually to enter the difficult game of
tying up supplies through bilateral deals, however, it would be entering with all the drawbacks of the latecomer. Its lack of experience
would likely make its early initiatives clumsy and ill-conceived. And its
late entry would mean that its negotiators would be canvassing a world
already thoroughly canvassed by Japan and others. In the first stages of
attempting to implement such a policy, the outcome would probably
be increased frustration rather than increased supplies of oil.

Problems of glut. It should not be supposed, however, that a prolonged period of glut will be an unmixed blessing for the United States.
The repercussions in terms of international relations would be particularly acute. Friendly countries such as Indonesia, Nigeria, Mexico,
Venezuela, and other oil exporters would be under increasing economic stress.

More to the point in the present context is the likelihood that in such
circumstances, despite the international implications, the United States
would impose new import restrictions on oil and its products. The
response of the U.S. oil industry to the shortage prospects of the 1970s
was to shift its exploration and development efforts out of unsafe areas
into more secure areas, especially out of Africa, Latin America, and the
Middle East to the North Sea, the North Slope, and the United States.
Moreover, there had been a surge of investment in other energy-gener-
ating undertakings, including gas, coal, secondary oil recovery operations, and synfuels. In the early 1980s, after a year or two of soft oil
prices, some of these efforts were abandoned, as governments cut back
their support and as business managers refused to accept the risks of
continued investment. But a considerable amount of high-cost oil
would probably continue to be produced. If so, it would be only a
matter of time before the U.S. government would be under great pressure to protect these relatively high-cost sources from cheap foreign
competition.[13]

In addition, the U.S. government might consider protecting production in safe areas outside the United States, such as the North Sea or even Mexico. Although the protection of such sources would entail some kind of discriminatory import regime on the part of the United States, it will be remembered that such arrangements had been developed on behalf of Canada and Mexico in the 1960s. Accordingly, in a sustained period of glut, a protected preferential energy regime is a real possibility.

If such a regime should develop, the emergence of the United States as a relatively high-cost energy source would once more appear as a possibility, with all the risks of impairing its competitive position that have already been mentioned. For lack of choice, Japan would be living off a glutted international oil market; although its long-run position would be insecure, its immediate situation would be that of the low-cost buyer. Meanwhile, inside their preferential area, the United States and its friends would be maintaining a higher price for oil than existed in the glutted markets of the world, and that fact, in turn, would lift other energy prices in the protected area. Once again, therefore, we are back to the possibilities of friction between the energy-using industries of the two countries.

Problems of endemic uncertainty. For some time to come, however, both the buyers and the sellers of oil and oil products will probably harbor substantial doubts about the long-term prospects of the industry. If both sides simultaneously fear for their long-term security, the question is whether they will respond with cooperative arrangements that are intended to reduce the risks to both. The obvious strategy, repeatedly observed in various industries in which the uncertainties are high, is for buyers and sellers to grope toward the reestablishment of some kind of vertical integration between them. Mutual uncertainties such as these are what continue to bind the Aramco companies to Saudi Arabia.

It must be emphasized that the reappearance and strengthening of vertical ties between buyers and sellers are conceivable only if uncertainty exists on both sides. If one side or the other were convinced that future market movements would favor its bargaining position, it would be unlikely to tie itself up with the long-term commitments that integration requires. But the conditions of mutual uncertainty did seem to exist as the 1980s began.

Sellers and buyers would be less disposed to look for integrative links, however, if they suspected that some of their competitors intended to resist the reintegration movement and to remain detached. A market characterized by a high degree of uncertainty and by a situation in which only some of the players were vertically integrated would be one of high risk for all.[14] In periods of glut, the integrated distributors would be at the mercy of the unintegrated distributors, who would be in a position to shop for bargains, whereas in periods of shortage, the unintegrated distributor would be exposed to danger from losing its sources of supply.

As far as the Japanese market is concerned, the possibility that domestic refiners and distributors might eventually be organized into some common structure for vertical linkage with their foreign sources of supply is not to be excluded. The Middle East and Indonesian sellers that supply most of the Japanese market are as uncertain as the distributors in Japan, whether multinational or national, over the future of prices and supplies. And although there is a possibility that some of the distributors in the Japanese market, especially some of the multinational distributors, might be unwilling or unable to return to an integrated structure, the risks of such a return in a market threatened by occasional glut may be mitigated by various factors. One is MITI's control over the market through its Petroleum Industry Law; the other is the Japanese practice of executing its oil-importing strategies through buying consortia in which the various distributors share.

As we saw in earlier chapters, Japan's experience with creating various complex forms of quasi-integration in order to establish claims on materials in periods of scarcity has been quite extensive, especially in coal, aluminum, copper, and iron ore. To be sure, the integration has been less than complete and it has generated less than total security for the buyers; but that weakness could be reduced a little by the geographic diversification of sources. The appearance of various forms of quasi-integration in the Japanese oil market, therefore, is not to be excluded.

The prospects for the U.S. market, however, are wholly different. We have already observed that a number of exporting countries, including notably Saudi Arabia and Venezuela, have felt obliged to weaken their links to the distribution systems of the multinational enterprises, not to strengthen them. Part of that trend has been the result of the oil-exporting countries' assumption that they faced a long period of oil shortages and hence had no acute need for the distribution facilities of the multinationals. With the development of much more uncertain prospects since then, one might expect that the policy of loosening those links would change; and indeed signs of such a change have appeared in some countries. But domestic political forces in these countries place some value on suppressing the institutions that they associate with the old era of dependency, a fact that creates greater problems for U.S. and European firms than for the Japanese. On the slightest showing of a return of shortages — even without such a showing in some cases — these forces are likely to reestablish a policy favoring a break from the multinationals' global distribution systems. The 40 percent or so of world oil trade that still lies within the vertically integrated systems of the multinational oil companies promises, in short, to shrink even further. The big international oil companies will also find it hard to rebuild their vertical links to the oil exporters because of the limitations on their ability to produce the necessary camouflage. Management contracts, such as the Japanese are accustomed to develop, serve that purpose much better than joint ventures. And package deals that involve broad commitments covering trade and technical flows serve the purpose much better than simpler deals that involve oil alone.

There are occasional signs that some multinationals, particularly the newer and smaller entrants such as Occidental Oil, have been trying to acquire the flexibility for mounting deals similar to those of the Japanese. Some of the exploration and development contracts that foreign oil companies have developed with various governments reflect a flexibility on the part of the companies that would have been improbable a decade age.[15] Nevertheless, in this respect the multinational oil companies cannot be expected to develop anything like the flexibility of the consortia created by Japanese interests. If the big international oil companies were to be willing to commit the necessary resources, most of them would still find it extraordinarily difficult to think in the terms needed for putting together the required deals. The organization and outlook of these oil firms have been shaped by decades of managing huge logistical systems such as oil fields, tanker fleets, and refineries; their habits of operation are not those of the financier and trader but those of the engineer — deliberate, rational, and cautious. The needed flexibility and improvisation would come with great difficulty from organizations such as these.

Overall, this analysis suggests that in a prolonged period of uncertainty, U.S. policy and Japanese policy with regard to oil may come out quite differently. U.S. policy will be shaped by three factors not present in Japan: the historical associations that handicap multinational enterprises when operating in developing countries, the existence of substantial supplies of "safe" oil and gas supplies in the United States, and the institutional inability of the country to put together complex deals. In combination, these factors still leave the U.S. economy a bit more secure than Japan in the short run — but at the price of draining its finite resources of oil at an accelerated rate. Meanwhile, the absence of these conditions in Japan may require it, whatever the risks, to live off the offerings of the international market. And if the rule of serendipity prevails once again, that inescapable need could in various plausible circumstances give Japan a lower-cost energy base than the United States.

Minerals and Metals

Elements of the oil story can be applied without great alteration to the various minerals and metals situations — but with numerous nuances and modifications.

For one thing, although all the projections, whether in energy or in metals, suffer from high degrees of uncertainty, the probabilities for shortages over the long term seem lower in metals than in oil. On the supply side, Japan's dogged efforts at stimulating the world supply of iron ore, copper, and bauxite — as well as coal and other minerals — offer some guarantee that any shortage of the common minerals will not persist for very long. On the demand side, the signs of increasing substitutability between the metals on the one hand and nonmetallic materials on the other, such as ceramics, optic fibers, and carbon fibers, also reduce the likelihood of shortage.

Another prospective difference between oil and the metals can be stated with much greater certainty: The prospects are slight for traumatic short-term interruptions in the supply of bauxite, iron ore, copper concentrates, and other commonly used minerals ores; and if such interruptions did occur, the threat of serious disturbance to the Japanese or the U.S. economy would not be great.[16] In the case of Japan, the conclusion is justified in part by the country's systematic use of national stockpiles as a buffering device. In the case of the United States, that conclusion also seems warranted, notwithstanding the fact that U.S. strategic stockpiles represent an altogether unreliable source for buffering the market in metals such as aluminum, copper, and steel. The lesser risks associated with these metals stem partly from the fact that the ores are not concentrated in vulnerable areas, as is oil in the Middle East. Japan does place fairly heavy reliance on Australia for metallic ores. But the possibility that Australian producers could exploit that dependence has been demonstrated by experience to be quite small. Besides, an interruption in the supply of raw materials to the metal producers is likely to be less disruptive than an interruption in the supply of oil to electric power plants or automobiles. In copper, for instance, the response to a short-term interruption would be partly for smelters to shift to copper scrap as a source of raw materials, partly for users to shift to aluminum as a substitute for copper, and partly for fabricators to postpone the manufacture of the products that use copper. If there is a prospective problem in the metals, therefore, it is with the implications for long-run imbalances rather than short-run disturbances.

Where long-run imbalances are concerned, the problem is as likely to be one of surplus as one of shortage. Where surpluses are involved, one precedent for U.S. policy is already at hand: that of steel, where the policy response has been to impose restrictions on imports. American steel firms, having failed to match the Japanese in their acquisition of low-cost foreign ores and having retreated to safer (and higher-cost) sources of raw materials, have added to their competitive handicaps and have demanded protection from cheaper foreign steel. A so-called trigger pricing mechanism has been applied to steel imports, increasing the U.S. price of steel. Copper, lead, and zinc producers have had similar recourse to protective devices at times in the past.

The U.S. economy has been rescued from a total commitment to such protective moves by the countervailing pressures of other groups in the economy. Users of copper, lead, and zinc have helped prevent the U.S. mining industry from limiting the importation of foreign ores and metals. And the chances are that, as such systems of restriction are proposed in the future, countervailing pressures may keep them in check. Yet it is still possible that the U.S. response may be predominantly one of protection.

Through all of these scenarios run several familiar themes. The Japanese government will think systematically about prospective national problems and will have some ability to act on the basis of its analyses. Sources in the United States may produce analyses as cogent and incisive, but the U.S. government will have neither the institutions nor the inclination to link analysis to action. In the Japanese case, official policies will bear some proximate relationship to the analysis that preceded them. In the U.S. case, declared policies are unlikely to lead for very long to actions consistent with the declarations.

Adding to the differences in the behavior of the two countries will be the nature of the links between government and enterprise. In the United States, the preference for an arm's-length relationship, which is deeply embedded in its institutions and ideological preferences, will greatly inhibit any sustained cooperative measures. In Japan, the problem of cooperation across the public-private frontier will remain much less acute.

Because of these profound differences in style of governance, the area for joint economic action between the two countries seems sharply circumscribed, being largely confined to self-denying ordinances such as agreements to remove barriers or reduce regulations. Such agreements may have some utility in relations between the two countries. But they will not help much in responding to the problems of long-term surplus or shortage.

Cooperation or Conflict?

We began with the wistful question of whether Japan and the United States might find themselves cooperating more extensively with each other as they confront their common problems in the acquisition of a dependable supply of raw materials. On the evidence, however, it seems fairly clear that cooperation between the two countries on any sustained and significant scale is unlikely. The efforts of various scholars who have sought earnestly to develop some constructive proposals for cooperation have generated mainly platitudes.[17] The national systems are extraordinarily disparate, to the point of incompatibility. Japan's penchant for explicit planning, for administrative guidance, and for collective national action could not be further from the norms and preferences of the United States. More relevant than the question of possible cooperation, therefore, is the question of possible friction.

The clashes between the United States and Japan that are suggested by these ruminations are not the stuff of which major political crises are made. Indeed, at worst, the problems foreseen in oil and metals, insofar as they suggest conflict, add up to little more than a set of quite ordinary headaches in the diplomatic agenda. Japan and the United States have become inured to their periodic spats over textiles, automobiles, oranges, and beef. If the automobile disputes of the early 1980s did not greatly imperil the bilateral ties of the two countries, it seems unlikely that the problems outlined here will do so.

The problems posed by raw materials are made manageable by various factors. One of these is the trend in the structure of the world's raw materials markets. Since 1916, when Lenin published his *Imperialism*, the markets for raw materials have become increasingly more dispersed and less subject to the control of producers. Although the world is still exposed to the risk of an interruption in the supply of oil from the Middle East, that risk is principally one of war or revolution; the possibility that the OPEC countries could agree to boycott any country, except perhaps the United States or Israel, is slight. And no analogous possibilities exist in the other principal metals analyzed here.

Moreover, in the past two decades, Japan has established a solid capacity to solve its problems of raw materials acquisition, a capacity that has added to the country's sense of self-confidence and has reduced its feeling of vulnerability. It is the U.S. capacity to do so, not the Japanese capacity, that is in question. In raw materials, as in many other cases of trade and investment involving the interests of the two countries, the United States is likely to see itself cast in the role of country bumpkin — unheeding before the fact, unprepared after it, and unable to learn from its experience. Where the interests of the two countries clash, the fact that the Japanese have their plans and policies under better control will be felt by some Americans as being vaguely unfair.

How, then, is the United States likely to behave if it is suffering from an acute shortage of a critical industrial material, while Japan seems adequately to have taken care of its needs? One cannot altogether exclude the possibility that the U.S. goverment may suddenly lash out in frustration, pushed to some ill-conceived action by ambitious bureaucrats, demagogic politicians, and an uninhibited press. The Nixon embargo on soy bean exports during the early 1970s is illustrative of such possibilities: a hasty measure, taken without much analysis of reflection.

But the soy bean case illustrates another abiding quality of the U.S. political process — the fact that it is extraordinarily difficult for the country to pursue any given course of action over a sustained period of time without reconsidering, qualifying, limiting, and reversing. The restrictions on exports of soy beans, in the end, lasted no more than ten weeks, as other sources of pressure in the American system exerted their influence.

The possibility that the U.S. government may take some ill-conceived measure, later to be reconsidered and modified, has been increased a little by its growing willingness to contemplate discriminatory actions in the trade field. Ideas of "reciprocity" and other such euphemisms for discrimination now come more readily to the minds of U.S. policy makers. The probability is increased even further by the fact that the preference of Japan's policy makers for an open trading system, however genuine that preference may be, does not run very deep and will no doubt show signs of flagging from time to time. In view of the overt discrimination being practiced by so many nations on Japanese exports, Japan's unwavering adherence to a nondiscriminatory open trading world would be little short of saintly.

Moreover, some of Japan's comprehensive trade and investment arrangements, such as those with the People's Republic of China or with the oil-exporting countries of the Middle East, cannot avoid being inherently discriminatory. If Japan is to give the assurances to these countries that they will be looking for, it will have to find ways of earmarking a portion of the Japanese market for the exports of those countries. In this respect, Japan will be doing no more than Germany has been obliged to do in agreeing to its mammoth gas deals with the Soviet Union, or Brazil in its deals with various countries of Africa and the Middle East; but in the context of a materials shortage, Japan's ability to arrange such deals could provoke special irritation.

Finally, apart from such relatively limited and explicit deals, there is the possibility that Japan may continue to flirt with more ambitious ideas for structuring new Southeast Asia trading arrangements, in some way involving Australia, China, and Japan's Southeast Asian trading partners.[18] The idea has so persistently surfaced and resurfaced in recent years that it cannot be dismissed out of hand, but the likelihood that any such idea would actually mature into a hard proposal is not very great. China and the Southeast Asian countries remain acutely wary of too close a tie with the Japanese; and Australia would have great difficulty developing special arrangements with Japan that would entail closer ties to Japan than to Europe and North America. Besides, until the Japanese government can find some way out of its contradictory desires to maintain a low military profile while holding off the

Soviet threat, it will be forced to handle its relations to the United States with great circumspection. These are the reasons, of course, why the innumerable conferences in which Japan has participated during the past decade on the concept of a Pacific community have produced nothing more than a succession of fatuous declarations.

The U.S. government, too, is reined in by numerous factors whenever it gives consideration to venting its frustrations on Japan: by its concern over the European security connection and its hope for a strong security link in the Pacific, by its desire to maintain agricultural exports, and by its various investment and technological links with Japanese interests. These factors may not always prevent the spokesmen and negotiators who purport to represent the U.S. position, including itinerant congressmen and cabinet officers, from taking uninhibited positions that contain an element of threat; but those positions are unlikely to prove very durable or consistent.

Still, despite the limited nature of the risks that these possibilities entail, there is good reason to try to hold those risks in check. For an American observer, it is natural enough to think first of what the U.S. side might conceivably do toward that end.

It goes without saying that measures taken by the United States to deal with its own supply problems, if done at Japanese expense, ought to be the subject of joint discussion. The most egregious of such provisions at the moment is the U.S. prohibition on the export of Alaskan oil; but either country is capable of such beggar-thy-neighbor measures. That a policy of restraint is needed with respect to such measures is too obvious for comment.

Nevertheless, the United States ought to be taking active measures to reduce its vulnerability to raw material dependence. Most of the elements of a sensible program for reducing such vulnerability have been known for a long time, having been laid out with care in the monumental Paley report in 1952.[19] Domestic stockpiles are needed, available in such quantities and on such terms as to meet short-term emergencies. In some cases, the construction and mothballing of processing facilities may be appropriate in order to be in a position to meet such emergencies. For materials that are threatened with scarcity over the long run, programs for the development of low-cost substitutes may be justified, especially where it appears that the private sector does not have the resources or the incentives to undertake such a program. Over the long term, the object of government policy should be to encourage the development of reserves in safe areas, including domestic sources. Over the decades, producing interests have consistently promoted the idea that more production in safe areas would automatically generate more reserves in safe areas. Where exhaustible resources such as oil and minerals are concerned, however, that self-serving concept has to be taken with a large pinch of salt. Instead, the government should be trying to find ways of developing reserves in safe areas under conditions that would defer their full exploitation until a time when they are actually needed. If such a policy were adopted, the size of domestic stockpiles would be determined in part by the length of time needed to bring the safe supplies on stream. Meanwhile, the government should be encouraging enterprises to draw their scarce materials from areas that might not be available over the long run, rather than from safe sources.

Will the U.S. government take any of these measures? In speculating on what it might do in the future, one cannot escape from the fact that the country's responses will be restrained by its own long history of relative security and success, and the ideologies these conditions have fostered. The U.S. system of governance and the country's ideological preferences were conceived and developed over several centuries during which the United States was plentifully supplied with its critical raw materials, was relatively isolated in economic terms, and was relatively safe in military terms. Besides, the underlying ideological preference of U.S. society to restrain the government's economic role seems for the moment stronger than ever. Eventually, new pressures on the American economy may affect some aspects of the country's ideology and habits of governance; but the changes will not come quickly. And until those pressures grow strong, the U.S. response to its raw material problems is likely to be constrained by these historical factors.[20]

If, despite such inhibitions, the U.S. government adopts an active policy along the suggested lines, it will open up various opportunities for collaboration with other countries. Even without any official policy on the U.S. side, U.S. enterprises have cooperated with those of Europe, Japan, and other countries in the joint development of scarce raw materials; various oil and mining operations, for instance, have brought enterprises from different home bases together in the same foreign operation. Measures of that sort may require little action from governments, apart from ensuring that mixed consortia will not be penalized for their polyglot character when they seek financial and political support from home governments. Some governments find that principle difficult to swallow, especially the French and the Japanese.

More generally, a number of countries might conceivably act as joint sponsors in programs to encourage an expansion of supplies of critical materials. In the first flush of official reactions over the oil crisis in the 1970s, the U.S. government and other governments made a few moves in that direction. As projects for the exploitation of deep sea minerals eventually begin to sharpen, multinational arrangements could reappear. If the U.S. government were to think in such terms, a partnership with Japan would not necessarily be the most obvious response; given the global character of U.S. interests, joint action with one or more European governments might be just as appropriate. But the possibility of joint ventures with Japan remains, especially because of Japan's rich experience in planning and supporting large-scale developmental projects.

In the atmosphere of the early 1980s, to be sure, the idea that the U.S. government might work with other governments to develop new sources of scarce materials has seemed fairly slight. The exchanges of the U.S. government with Europe and Japan over economic matters were being conducted with a special tone of acerbity and recrimination. But even that phase could pass, especially if these countries faced common economic shortages or common political threats.

Sharing between Japan and the United States remains a possibility primarily because it is so difficult to picture a set of events in the future that would effectively reduce the interdependence between them. Japan appears to have few options other than to live alongside the United States, even if in constant discomfiture. Except for the possibility of a sporadic unfriendly gesture, the United States is unlikely to block Japan's choice to remain in the American camp, as long as the Japanese elect to remain there. The two countries seem doomed to continue as the odd couple, sharing little in habits, values, and aspirations, yet unable to make any other choice but to accommodate themselves to one another's existence.

APPENDIX
NOTES
INDEX

APPENDIX: Statistics on the Importation and Consumption of Raw Materials

Table A.1. Imports as percent of apparent consumption in Japan and the United States, four industrial raw materials, 1955, 1970, and 1979.

Product[a]	Japan			United States		
	1955	1970	1979	1955	1970	1979
Petroleum	95.9	99.5	99.8	11.6	21.9	44.3
Iron ore	84.7	99.1	99.6[b]	19.2	34.7	30.1
Bauxite and alumina	100.0	100.0	100.0	52.7	65.2	69.8
Copper ore and materials	37.7	80.47	98.7	34.0	15.2	6.4

a. Petroleum includes crude oil and products in crude oil equivalents for the United States, but crude oil only for Japan. Iron ore includes concentrates. Alumina is calculated in bauxite equivalents. Copper materials, including concentrates, matte, and blister, are calculated in ore equivalents.

b. 1978 data.

Sources: Library of Congress, Congressional Research Service, *Energy Factbook* (Washington, D.C.: Government Printing Office, 1980); John C. McCaslin, ed., *International Petroleum Encyclopedia, 1981*, vol. 14 (Tulsa, Oklahoma: PennWell Publishing Co., 1981); Sukeyuki Kawata, ed., *Japan's Iron and Steel Industry* (Tokyo: Tokyo Foreign Service, 1958, 1970); Willy Bauer, ed., *Metal Statistics* (Frankfurt: Metallgesellschaft, 52nd ed. 1955–64, 67th ed. 1969–79); United Nations, *World Energy Supplies, 1950–1974* (New York, 1976); United Nations, *1979 Yearbook of International Trade Statistics*, vol. 2 (New York, 1980); United Nations, *1979 Yearbook of World Energy Statistics* (New York, 1980); U.S. Bureau of Mines, *Minerals Yearbook*, vol. 1 (Washington, D.C.: Government Printing Office, 1955, 1971, and 1978–79).

Note: Figures of the sort contained in this table require that the compiler make arbitrary decisions, such as the extent to which imports of the raw materials embodied in processed forms should be included. Accordingly, figures of this sort vary considerably from different sources. The general trends from these different sources, however, are similar.

Table A.2. Relative position of Japan and the United States in world consumption a importation of four industrial raw materials, 1955, 1970, and 1979.

	Percent of world totals[a]								
	Japan			United States			Other countries		
	1955	1970	1979	1955	1970	1979	1955	1970	197
Apparent consumption									
Crude and refined petro-leum products[b]	1	10	11	62	35	35	37	55	54
Iron ore	3	20	29[d]	48	25	22[d]	49	55	49
Bauxite[c]	2	12	14	61	44	40	37	44	46
Copper ore	3	10	14	37	29	22	60	61	64
Imports									
Crude and refined petro-leum products[b]	3	14	14	17	12	23	80	74	63
Iron ore	8	39	38	34	16	14	58	45	48
Bauxite[c]	3	10	9	47	49	42	50	41	49
Copper ore	12	79	75	26	7	3	62	14	22

a. The U.S.S.R., Eastern Europe, and the People's Republic of China are excluded fro all totals in the table. In addition, Taiwan is excluded from statistics on petroleum.

b. Data covering crude oil alone show only minor differences.

c. Includes alumina imports measured in bauxite content.

d. 1978 data.

Sources: American Metal Market, *Metal Statistics 1981* (New York: Fairchild Public tions, 1981); U.K. Iron and Steel Statistics Bureau, *International Steel Statistics: Summa Tables* (London, 1979); Willy Bauer, ed., *Metal Statistics* (Frankfurt: Metallgesellschaf 52nd ed. 1955–1964, and 68th ed. 1970–1980); National Commission on Materials Polic *Toward a National Materials Policy, World Perspective: Second Interim Repo* (Washington, D.C.: Government Printing Office, 1973); United Nations, *World Energ Supplies, 1950–1974* (New York, 1976); United Nations, *1979 Yearbook of Internation Trade Statistics*, vol. 2 (New York, 1980); United Nations, *1979 Yearbook of World Energ Statistics* (New York, 1980).

Table A.3. Herfindahl indexes of concentration of world production in three industries.[a]

Industry	Year	Index
Copper		
Copper ore production	1950	.100
	1960	.074
	1970	.046
	1980	.046
Copper-refining capacity	1950	.071
	1960	.058
	1970	.050
	1980	.035
Iron and steel		
Iron ore production	1950	.047
	1957	.036
	1964	.021
	1970	.022
	1979	.043
Crude steel production	1950	.039
	1960	.020
	1967	.015
	1976	.021
	1979	.022
Aluminum		
Bauxite production	1948	.266
	1960	.105
	1969	.111
	1973	.126
Primary aluminum-smelting capacity	1950	.181
	1955	.147
	1960	.114
	1965	.095
	1970	.092
	1975	.059

a. Communist countries are omitted.

Sources: COPPER AND COPPER ORE: American Bureau of Metal Statistics, *Non-Ferrous Metal Data 1980* (New York, 1981); idem, *Yearbook 1950, 1960, and 1970* (New York, 1951, 1961, 1971); Willy Bauer, ed., *Metal Statistics* (Frankfurt: Metallgesellschaft, 47th ed. 1950–59, 57th ed. 1960–69, 68th ed. 1970–1980). STEEL: American Metal Market, *Metal Statistics* (New York: Fair-

Table A.3. (continued)

child Publications, 1952, 1961, 1968, and 1980); *Iron and Steel Works of the World* (London: Metal Bulletin Books, 1st ed. 1952, 3rd ed. 1962, 5th ed. 1969, and 6th ed. 1974); *Moody's Industrial Manual* (New York: Moody's Investors Service, 1952, 1962, and 1968). IRON ORE: U.S. Bureau of Mines, *Minerals Yearbook* (Washington, D.C.: Government Printing Office, 1950, 1957, 1964, 1970, and 1979); United Nations, *The World Market for Iron Ore* (New York, 1968). ALUMINUM: United Nations, Center on Transnational Corporations, *Transnational Corporations in World Development: A Re-examination* (New York, 1978), p. 261; American Bureau of Metal Statistics, *Non-Ferrous Metal Data 1975* (New York, 1976), pp. 91-96; idem, *Yearbook 1960* (New York, 1961), pp. 92-94. BAUXITE: First Boston Corporation, *Aluminum: The Industry and the Four North American Producers* (New York, 1951), p. 13; Walter C. Labys, *Market Structure, Bargaining Power, and Resource Price Formation* (Lexington, Mass.: D.C. Heath, 1980), p. 142; U.S. Bureau of Mines, *Minerals Yearbook* (Washington, D.C.: Government Printing Office, 1950, 1961, 1970, and 1974); Douglas W. Woods and James C. Burrows, *The World Aluminum-Bauxite Market* (New York: Praeger, 1980), p. 71.

Note: The formula for the Herfindahl index is:

$$H = \sum_{i=1}^{n} s_i^2$$

where n = the number of firms in the industry, and s_i = the market share of the ith firm.

NOTES

1. Partners or Rivals

1. A classic source is V. I. Lenin, *Imperialism, The Highest State of Capitalism* (Moscow: Progress Publishers, 15th printing 1970). For a review of the issue in international relations, see Pierre Renouvier and J. B. Durosell, *Introduction to the History of International Relations* (New York: Praeger, 1964), ch. 1; also D. A. Deese, "Oil, War and Grand Strategy," *Orbis*, no. 3 (Fall 1981): 525–556.

2. See John Dower, "Occupied Japan and the American Lake, 1945–1950," in Edward Friedman and Mark Selden, eds., *America's Asia: Dissenting Essays on Asian-American Relations* (New York: Pantheon, 1969), pp. 146–206; and Jon Livingston, Joe Moore, and Felicia Oldfather, eds., *Postwar Japan: 1945 to the Present* (New York: Random House, 1973), pp. 106–138.

3. See, for example, I. M. Destler, *Managing an Alliance: The Politics of U.S.-Japanese Relations* (Washington, D.C.: Brookings Institution, 1976), pp. 114–119.

4. D. B. Keesing and Martin Wolf, *Textile Quotas Against Developing Countries* (London: Trade Policy Research Centre, 1980), p. 15; also D. B. Yoffie, "The Newly Industrializing Countries and the Political Economy of Protectionism," *International Studies Quarterly* 25, no. 4 (December 1981): 575.

5. Michael Blaker, *The Politics of Trade: U.S. and Japanese Policymaking for the GATT Negotiations* (New York: Columbia University Press, 1978), pp. 2–7; I. M. Destler, Haruhiro Fukui, and Hideo Sato, *The Textile Wrangle: Conflict in Japanese-American Relations, 1969–1971* (Ithaca, N.Y.: Cornell University Press, 1979), pp. 28–36; Warren S. Hunsberger, *Japan and the United States in World Trade* (New York: Harper and Row, 1964), pp.

234–237, 329–333; also John Lynch, *Toward an Orderly Market* (Tokyo; Sophia University, 1968), pp. 180–188.

6. "Putting the Heat on Japan," *The Economist*, August 28, 1971, pp. 37–38; "Japan: The Year of the Shock," *Asian Survey* 12, no. 1 (January 1972): 46–52; Destler, *Managing an Alliance*, pp. 35–45.

7. The shift in roles is well described in L. B. Krause and Sueo Sekiguchi, eds., *Economic Interaction in the Pacific Basin* (Washington, D.C.: Brookings Institution, 1980), pp. 23–78.

8. See, for instance, MITI, *White Paper on International Trade* (Tokyo: Japan External Trade Organization, 1973), pp. 24–25, 39.

9. Saburo Okita, *Japan in the World Economy* (Tokyo: Japan Foundation, 1975), pp. 219–220; John K. Emmerson and Daniel I. Okimoto, "The U.S.-Japan Alliance: Overview and Outlook," in U. Alexis Johnson and George R. Packard, eds., *The Common Security Interests of Japan, the United States, and NATO* (Cambridge, Mass.: Ballinger, 1981), p. 97.

10. For a review of the 1982 measures, see "Government Making All-Out Effort to Remove Non-Tariff Barriers," *Journal of Japanese Trade and Industry* 1, no. 2 (1982): 6, 10–13. For a Japanese view that such reforms are still superficial, see Soji Teramura, "Fake Market – Opening Measures Will Not Pass Muster," *Economic Eye* 3, no. 2 (June 1982): 19–22, translated from *Chuo Koron* , May 1982.

11. Masamichi Hanabusa, *Trade Problems Between Japan and Western Europe* (New York: Praeger, 1979), p. 3; G. H. Perlow, "The Multilateral Supervision of International Trade: Has the Textiles Experiment Worked?" *American Journal of International Law* 75 (1981): 93–133; Keesing and Wolf, *Textile Quotas Against Developing Countries*.

12. J. A. Finlayson and M. W. Zadier, "The GATT and the Regulation of Trade Barriers: Regime Dynamics and Functions," *International Organization* 35, no. 4 (Autumn 1981): 568.

13. Finlayson and Zadier, "The GATT and the Regulation of Trade Barriers," pp. 568, 581–584; "Legal Guide to the Tokyo Round," *Journal of World Trade Law* 13, no. 5 (September-October 1979): 443–444.

14. See OECD, *East-West Trade: Recent Developments in Countertrade* (Paris, 1981); and OECD, *Countertrade Practices in East-West Economic Relations* (Paris, 1979).

15. M. A. Maggiotto and E. R. Wittkopf, "American Public Attitudes Toward Foreign Policy," *International Studies Quarterly* 25, no. 4 (December 1981): 601–631; also Council on Foreign Relations, *New Directions in U.S. Foreign Policy* (New York, 1981); and Cambridge Reports, Inc., *The Emerging Consensus: Public Attitudes on America's Ability to Compete in the World*, prepared for Union Carbide, Inc., New York, January 1981.

16. S. D. Krasner, "The Tokyo Round: Particularistic Interests and Prospects for Stability in the Global Trading System," *International Studies Quarterly* 23, no. 4 (December 1979): 515; Finlayson and Zadier, "The GATT and the Regulation of Trade Barriers," p. 569n.

17. Tomosaburo Yoshimine, "Settlement Finally Reached for NTT Procure-

ment Issue," *Business Japan* 3 (1981): 75–77.

18. "Reagan Requests $128 Million Help for El Salvador," *New York Times*, March 18, 1982, pp. A1–A13.

19. "Caribbean Aid Effort Encounters Protectionist Trouble in Congress," *New York Times*, May 7, 1982, p. A8. An article that does address the basic principle, however, is R. E. Feinberg and R. S. Newfarmer, "A Bilateralist Gamble," *Foreign Policy*, no. 47 (Summer 1982): 133–138.

20. "Free Trade Stressed by U.S.," *New York Times*, July 8, 1981, p. D2; "Washington's Trade War of Words," *Fortune*, April 5, 1982, pp. 35–39; "Japan's Trade War with the West Goes from Cold to Hot," *The Economist*, April 24, 1982, p. 87.

21. GATT, *International Trade 1980/81* (Geneva, 1981), p. 2.

22. Raymond Vernon, *Storm Over the Multinationals* (Cambridege, Mass.: Harvard University Press, 1978), pp. 2–5.

23. For an analysis of the performance of U.S.-based firms, see Gerald K. Helleiner and Real Lavergne, "Intra-Firm Trade and Industrial Exports to the United States," *Oxford Bulletin of Economics and Statistics* 41, no. 4 (November 1979): 297–311.

24. O. G. Whichard, "Employment and Employee Compensation of U.S. Multinational Corporations in 1977," *Survey of Current Business*, February 1982, p. 38.

25. For instance, Kiyoshi Kojima, *Japan and a New World Order* (Boulder, Colo.: Westview Press, 1977), pp. 75–82.

26. For a comparison of Japanese and U.S. multinationals, see Hideki Yoshihara, "Japanese Multinational Enterprises: A View from Outside," *Kobe Economic and Business Review*, 25th Annual Report, Kobe University, 1979, pp. 15–35.

27. Louis T. Wells, Jr., *Third World Multinationals* (Cambridge, Mass.: MIT Press, forthcoming).

28. MITI, *Gaishikei Kigyo no doko* [Foreign Business Affiliates in Japan] (Tokyo, 1980), reprinted in Mary Saso, "Japanese Industry," Economist Intelligence Unit Special Report 110, London, October 1981, p. 75.

29. *Survey of Current Business*, August 1981, p. 4.

30. Hokaji Mino, "Auto Exports Create Further Discord," *Business Japan*, no. 1 (1982): 28.

31. Naohiro Amaya, "Grumblings of a Shop-Clerk of Japan, a Tradesman's Country," translated from *Bungei Shunju*, March 1980; Masamori Sase, "Rejection of 'Tradesman's Nation' Argument," from *Bungei Shunju*, April 1980. Also Kazuo Nukazawa, "Whither Japan's Foreign Economic Policy? Straws in the Wind," *The World Economy* 1, no. 4 (February 1980): 467–480.

32. Michael Nacht and Mike Mochizuki, "Modes of Defense Cooperation Between the United States and Japan," *Annual Report*, U.S.–Japan Program, Center for International Affairs, Harvard University, 1982.

33. For an excellent review, see Gerald Curtis, "Japanese Security Policies and the United States," *Foreign Affairs* 59, no. 4 (Spring 1981): 852–874; Donald C. Hellmann, "Japanese Security and Postwar Japanese Foreign

Policy," in Robert A. Scalapino, ed., *The Foreign Policy of Japan* (Berkeley: University of California Press, 1977), pp. 321–340; and Makato Momoi, "Basic Trends in Japanese Security Policies," ibid., pp. 341–364.

34. "U.S. is Fashioning New Military Strategy for Asia," *New York Times*, June 7, 1982, p. A3.

35. E. O. Reischauer, *Japan* (New York: Knopf, 1974), pp. 107–110, 297–299, 336–338; and C. G. Cleaver, *Japanese and Americans: Cultural Parallels and Paradoxes* (Minneapolis: University of Minnesota Press, 1976), pp. 9–10, 231–234. Chie Nakane, *Japanese Society* (Berkeley: University of California Press, 1970), provide an extensive exploration of the elements that make for this sense of identity and distinctiveness.

36. A typical view appears in Nagai Yonosuke, "Defense of a Moratorium State," *Japan Echo* 8, no. 2 (1982): 7–81, translated and abridged from "Moratoriamu Kokka no boei ron," *Chuo Koron*, January 1981, pp. 74–108; and in Isamu Miyazaki, "Economic Prosperity or a Strong Military?" *Economic Eye* 3, no. 1 (March 1982): 4–12.

37. See, for instance, "Weinberger Asks Japanese to Rearm," *New York Times*, March 26, 1982, p. 3.

38. Nacht and Mochizuki, "Modes of Defense Cooperation Between the United States and Japan."

39. See, for instance, "Japan's Top Leaders Express View on Comprehensive Security," *Business Japan*, no. 4 (1982): 19–31.

40. "Report on Comprehensive National Security," July 2, 1980, quoted in R. A. Morse, "Energy and Japan's National Security Strategy," in Morse, *The Politics of Japan's Energy Strategy* (Berkeley: University of California Press, 1981), p. 55.

41. See, for instance, Flora Lewis, "Alarm Bells in the West," *Foreign Affairs* 60, no. 3 (1982): 551–572; also "Snow Right and Europe," *The Economist*, February 27, 1982, pp. 11–12; and, in the same issue, "Alliance Ailments," pp. 17–23.

42. John E. Rielly, ed., *U.S. Public Opinion and American Foreign Policy* (Chicago: Chicago Council on Foreign Relations, 1979).

43. Krause and Sekiguchi, *Economic Interaction in the Pacific Basin*, pp. 259–262.

44. See Mitsuro Donowaki, "The Pacific Basin Community: The Evolution of a Concept," *Speaking of Japan* 2, no. 15 (March 1982): pp. 23–32.

2. The World Oil Market in Transition

1. John Blair, *The Control of Oil* (New York: Pantheon, 1976), pp. 159–164; Federal Trade Commission, *The International Petroleum Cartel*, U.S. Senate, Select Committee on Small Business, 82nd Cong., 2nd Sess. (Washington, D.C.: Government Printing Office, 1952), rpt. Arno Press, 1976, pp. 163–190.

2. Blair, *The Control of Oil*, pp. 63–71.

3. Elements of the structure went back even earlier. See Edith T. Penrose, *The Large International Firm in Developing Countries* (London: Allen and Unwin, 1968), pp. 178–185.

4. But see Federal Trade Commission, *The International Petroleum Cartel*, pp. 352–370; Wayne A. Leeman, *The Price of Middle East Oil* (Ithaca, N.Y.: Cornell University Press, 1962), pp. 84–115; Helmut J. Frank, *Crude Oil Prices in the Middle East* (New York: Praeger, 1966), pp. 7–115.

5. Federal Trade Commission, *The International Petroleum Cartel*, pp. 275–346.

6. See, for instance, Benjamin Shwadran, *The Middle East, Oil and the Great Powers* (New York: Halsted Press, 1973), p. 539.

7. J. E. Hartshorn, *Politics and World Oil Economics* (New York: Praeger, 1962), p. 107.

8. See, for instance, O. E. Williamson, *Markets and Hierarchies: Analysis and Antitrust Implications* (New York: Free Press, 1975), pp. 82–131; D. L. Kaserman, "Theories of Vertical Integration: Implications for Antitrust Policy," *Antitrust Bulletin* 23, no. 3 (Fall 1978): 483–510.

9. For the role of vertical integration in the international oil industry, see M. A. Adelman, *The World Petroleum Industry* (Baltimore: Johns Hopkins University Press, 1972), pp. 89–100; D. J. Teece, "Vertical Integration in the U.S. Oil Industry," in E. J. Mitchell, ed., *Vertical Integration in the Oil Industry* (Washington, D.C.: American Enterprise Institute, 1976), pp. 83–89, 116–117; Penrose, *The Large International Firm in Developing Countries*, pp. 150–172; and Brian Levy, "World Oil Marketing in Transition," *International Organization* 36, no. 1 (Winter 1982): 113–134.

10. For a sampling of views, see, for instance, D. A. Rustow and J. F. Mugno, *OPEC: Success and Prospects* (New York: New York University Press, 1976), esp. pp. 1–32; A. D. Johany, *The Myth of the OPEC Cartel: The Role of Saudi Arabia* (New York: Wiley, 1980), pp. 33–53; Ian Seymour, *OPEC: Instrument of Change* (New York: St. Martin's, 1981); and Raymond Vernon, ed., *The Oil Crisis* (New York: Norton, 1976), p. 6, introduction. An extremely well-balanced and informed description of OPEC's role appears in J. E. Hartshorn, "Two Crises Compared: OPEC Pricing in 1973–1975 amd 1978–1980," in Ragaei el Mallakh, *OPEC: Twenty Years and Beyond* (Boulder, Colo: Westview Press, 1982), pp. 17–32.

11. R. C. Weisberg, *The Politics of Crude Oil Pricing in the Middle East, 1970–1975* (Berkeley: Institute of International Studies, 1977), pp. 37–51.

12. Rustow and Mugno, *OPEC: Success and Prospects*, pp. 130–131.

13. Fariborz Ghadar, *The Evolution of OPEC Strategy* (Lexington, Mass.: Lexington Books, 1977), pp. 35–46.

14. The events are well chronicled in J. E. Hartshorn, "Two Crises Compared," pp. 18–26.

15. See, for instance, "First Split in OPEC Pricing Unity," *Petroleum Economist* 44, no. 1 (January 1977): 2; "Competition Cuts 1978 OPEC Output," *Petroleum Economist* 46, no. 1 (January 1979): 5; "Widening OPEC Differentials," *Petroleum Economist* 46, no. 2 (February 1979): 65. For 1981–82, see "Market Trends," *Petroleum Economist* 49, no. 4 (April 1982): 160; and "OPEC Moves to Defend Prices," ibid., p. 122. Although sponsored by OPEC itself, Ian Seymour's *OPEC: Instrument of Change* contains a fairly dispassionate

recapitulation of OPEC decisions; his evaluations of OPEC's role, however, differ from mine.

16. See, for instance, "OPEC Agonistes," *The Economist*, January 23, 1982, p. 59.

17. Estimated from Petroleum Economics, Ltd., *Oil Industry Development* (London: January-February 1978 to May-June 1980).

18. Estimated from published sources by Exxon International, photocopy, February 11, 1980.

19. For Venezuela, see Alirio A. Parra, "The New Role of National Oil Companies," *Middle East Economic Survey* 23, no. 47 (September 8, 1980): 5; for Nigeria, Øystein Noreng, "State Trading and the Politics of Oil," in M. M. Kostecki, ed., *State Trading in International Markets* (London: Macmillan, 1982), p. 112.

20. "Denmark — State Oil Company," *Oil Industry Developments*, January-February 1980, p. 48.

21. *The Economist*, January 23, 1982, p. 34 advertisement.

22. George W. Grayson, *The Politics of Mexican Oil* (Pittsburgh: University of Pittsburgh, 1980), pp. 177–179.

23. George W. Grayson, "Oil and Politics in Mexico," *Current History* 80 no. 469 (November 1981): 382.

24. This development is a central theme in M. A. Conant, *The Oil Factor in U.S. Policy, 1980–1990* (Lexington, Mass.: D. C. Heath, 1982), pp. 91–92.

25. *Shell Polymers* 6, no. 1 (1982): 3–4.

26. The behavior of such stocks since 1973 is hard to interpret, probably reflecting such ambivalence. On U.S. inventory data, see *Twentieth Century Petroleum Statistics* (Dallas: De Golyer and MacNaughton, November 1981), pp. 57, 65.

27. "Saudi Arabia Buys a Japanese Maccano Set," *The Economist*, April 22, 1981, p. 53; "European Petrochemicals: End of an Era," *The Economist*, December 19, 1981, p. 64; and "Oil Refining: A Scrap Metal Business," ibid., p. 65.

28. See, for instance, "A New Chemical Triangle Takes Shape in Arabia," *The Economist*, February 7, 1981, p. 71.

29, "Kuwait to Buy Santa Fe for $2.5 Billion," *Oil and Gas Journal*, October 12, 1981, pp. 56–57.

3. Changing World Markets in Minerals and Metals

1. Brief descriptions of the market structures for bauxite, iron ore, and copper ore appear in W. C. Labys, "The Role of State Trading in Mineral Commodity Markets," in M. M. Kostecki, ed., *State Trading in International Markets* (London: Macmillan, 1982), pp. 78–102.

2. W. C. Labys, *Market Structure, Bargaining Power, and Resource Price Formation* (Lexington, Mass.: Lexington Books, 1980), pp. 6–23.

3. Dani Rodrik, "Changing Patterns of Ownership and Integration in the Bauxite-Aluminum Industry," in Leroy P. Jones, ed., *Public Enterprise in Less-*

Developed Countries: Multidisciplinary Perspectives (Cambridge: Cambridge University Press, 1982), forthcoming.

4. Calculated from Labys, *Market Structure, Bargaining Power, and Resource Price Information*, Table 5-8, p. 156.

5. G. W. Stocking and M. W. Watkins, *Cartels in Action* (New York: Twentieth Century Fund, 1947), pp. 46-247.

6. Ervin Hexner, *International Cartels* (Chapel Hill: University of North Carolina Press, 1946), pp. 203-215.

7. Walter Adams and Joel B. Dirlam, "Big Steel, Invention, and Innovation," *Quarterly Journal of Economics* 80, no. 2 (May 1966): 167-189.

8. Alex Skelton, "Copper," in William Y. Elliott et al., *International Control in the Non-Ferrous Metals* (New York: Macmillan, 1937), p. 501; and J. L. McCarthy, "The American Copper Industry, 1947-1955," *Yale Economic Essays* 4, no. 1 (Spring 1964): 65-130.

9. Raymond Vernon and Brian Levy, "State-Owned Enterprises in the World Economy: The Case of Iron Ore," in Jones, ed., *Public Enterprise in Less-Developed Countries*, forthcoming.

10. Rodrik, "Changing Patterns of Ownership and Integration in the Bauxite-Aluminum Industry."

11. The U.S. figure is from National Research Council, *A Century of Doctorates* (Washington, D.C., 1978), p. 47. The European figure is from UNESCO, *Statistics of Students Abroad* (Paris, 1976), Table 6.

12. *Metals Week* 48, no. 26 (June 27, 1977): 9.

13. Vernon and Levy, "State-Owned Enterprises in the World Economy: The Case of Iron Ore."

14. "1958 Outlook: Copper," *Engineering and Mining Journal* 159, no. 2 (February 1958): 115. The record in *Reading Industries v. Kennecott Copper Corporation et al.*, U.S. District Court for the Southern District of New York, June 12, 1979, contains considerable detail on efforts to fix copper prices.

15. Wolfgang Glushke, Joseph Shaw, and Benison Varon, *Copper: The Next Fifteen Years* (Dordrecht, Holland: D. Reidel, 1979), p. xxvi; John Tilton, *Future of Non-Fuel Minerals* (Washington, D.C.: Brookings Institution, 1977), p. 52; "Copper: How Long, Oh Lord?" *Forbes*, February 20, 1978, p. 79.

16. Rodrik, "Changing Patterns of Ownership and Integration in the Bauxite-Aluminum Industry."

17. OECD, *Problems and Prospects of the Primary Aluminum Industry* (Paris, 1973), p. 42.

18. C. J. Maule and I. A. Litvak, "The International Bauxite Agreement: A Commodity Cartel in Action," *International Affairs*, Spring 1980, pp. 296-314.

19. Vernon and Levy, "State-Owned Enterprises in the World Economy: The Case of Iron Ore."

20. Labys, "The Role of State Trading in Mineral Commodity Markets," p. 99.

21. Vernon and Levy, "State-Owned Enterprises in the World Economy: The Case of Iron Ore."

22. Ibid.

23. GATT, *International Trade 1980–81* (Geneva, 1980–81), p. 19.

24. Economic Commission for Latin America, "Negotiating Capacity of Latin America Governments vis-à-vis Transnational Corporations in Export Oriented Primary Commodities," for presentation at Bangkok, October 8, 1979, p. 19.

25. Ibid., p. 20.

26. Marian Radetzki, *Mineral Processing in Developing Countries*, U.N. Industrial Development Organization (Vienna, 1980), p. 92.

27. "Codelco-Chile is Looking for European Partners," *Metals Week*, August 13, 1979, p. 7.

28. "Codelco Has Signed a Tolling Contract," *Metals Week*, February 25, 1980, p. 6.

29. See "Tin Market Uncertainty Benefits the Malaysians," *New York Times*, March 29, 1982, p. D1; on Brazilian coffee manipulations of 1980, see "Coffee Producers Price Propping Ploys Slip on Big Crops, Slump in Consumption," *Wall Street Journal*, August 27, 1980, p. 28.

30. See Stephan Fay, *Beyond Greed: The Hunts and Their Silver Bubble* (New York: Viking, 1982).

4. American Principles and Practices

1. For a summary of this theme and other principal themes in the interpretation of American political behavior, see S. P. Huntington, *American Politics: The Promise of Disharmony* (Cambridge, Mass.: Harvard University Press, 1981), pp. 5–12.

2. See for instance, L. C. Thurow, *The Zero Sum Society: Distribution and the Possibilities for Economic Change* (New York: Basic Books, 1980); J. A. Pechman, ed., *Setting National Priorities for the 1980s* (Washington, D.C.: Brookings Institution, 1980): R. L. Heilbroner and L. C. Thurow, *Five Economic Challenges* (Englewood Cliffs, N.J.: Prentice-Hall, 1981); J. A. Califano, Jr., *Governing America: An Insider's Report from Washington* (New York: Simon and Schuster, 1981); B. J. Heineman, Jr., and C. A. Hessler, *Memorandum to the President: A Strategic Approach to Domestic Affairs in the 1980s)* (New York: Random House, 1980); W. A. Rosenbaum, *Energy, Politics and Public Policy* (Washington, D.C.: Congressional Quarterly Press, 1981), pp. 69–71.

3. Comparative statements of this general tenor are fairly common; see, for instance, J. D. Aberbach, R. D. Putnam, and B. A. Rockman, *Bureaucrats and Politicians in Western Democracies* (Cambridge, Mass.: Harvard University Press, 1981), pp. 22–23.

4. The cyclical hypotheses are summarized in Huntington, *American Politics*, pp. 148–149.

5. On this aspect see S. D. Krasner, *Defending the National Interest* (Princeton, N.J.: Princeton University Press, 1978), pp. 61–69; Louis Hartz, *The Liberal Tradition in America* (New York: Harcourt, Brace and World, 1955), pp. 43–44.

6. R. E. Neustadt, *Presidential Power: The Politics of Leadership* (New York: Wiley, 1980), pp. 7–8.

7. See Andrew Shonfield, *Modern Capitalism: The Changing Balance of Public and Private Power* (London: Oxford University Press, 1965), pp. 305–307; David E. Wilson, *The National Planning Idea in U.S. Public Policy: Five Alternative Approaches* (Boulder, Colo: Westview Press, 1980), p. 25; and Stephen D. Krasner, "United States Commercial and Monetary Policy: Unravelling the Paradox of External Strength and Internal Weakness," in Peter J. Katzenstein, ed., *Between Power and Plenty: Foreign Economic Policies of Advanced Industrial States* (Madison: University of Wisconsin Press, 1979), pp. 51–87.

8. See, for instance, L. D. Epstein, *Political Parties in Western Democracies* (New York: Praeger, 1967), pp. 193–198; R. A. Alford, *Party and Society: The Anglo-American Democracies* (Chicago: Rand McNally, 1973), pp. 94–122, 219–248, 309–318; W. N. Chambers, "Parties and Nation Building in America," in Joseph La Palombara and Myron Weiner, eds., *Political Parties and Political Development* (Princeton, N.J.: Princeton University Press, 1966), p. 83.

9. *Schechter Corp.* v. *U.S.*, 495 U.S. 541, 1935.

10. Quoted in Walter Salant, "The Collected Writings of John Maynard Keynes," *Journal of Economic Literature* 17, no. 3 (September 1980): 1058.

11. See, for instance, Potter Stewart, "Or of the Press," *Hastings Law Journal* 26, no. 3 (January 1975): 631–637; G. L. Waples, "The Freedom of Information Act: A Seven-Year Assessment," *Columbia Law Review* 74 (June 1974): 895–959; R. B. Stewart, "The Reformation of American Administrative Law," *Harvard Law Review* 88, no. 8 (June 1975): 1667; Rosenbaum, *Energy, Politics and Public Policy*, pp. 89–93.

12. See, for instance, M. J. Marks, "Remedies to 'Unfair' Trade," *The World Economy* 1, no. 2 (January 1978): 223–236; also C. J. Green, "Legal Protectionism in the United States and Its Impact on United States–Japan Economic Relations," unpublished report to the Advisory Group on United States–Japan Economic Relations, July 1980.

13. Robert S. Gilmour, "The Congressional Veto," *Journal of Policy Analysis and Management* 2, no. 1 (Fall 1982): 13–25.

14. Ibid., pp. 16–20.

15. W. D. Burnham, "The Onward March of Party Decomposition," and Philip E. Converse, "The Erosion of Party Fidelity," in R. G. Niemi and F. Weisberg, eds., *Controversies in American Voting Behavior* (San Francisco: W. H. Freeman, 1976), pp. 422–488.

16. Morris P. Fiorina, *Congress: Keystone of the Washington Establishment* (New Haven: Yale University Press, 1977), pp. 23–28.

17. See, for instance, Henry Jacoby, *The Bureaucratization of the World* (Berkeley: University of California Press, 1973), pp. 26–85.

18. For evidence that such administrators tend to come disproportionately from upper-middle-income families, see, for instance, Hugh Heclo, *A Government of Strangers: Executive Politics in Washington* (Washington, D.C.: Brookings Institution, 1977), pp. 114–115.

19. Aberbach, Putnam, and Rockman, *Bureaucrats and Politicians in Western Democracies*, pp. 94-96.

20. See, for instance, R. J. Hrebenar and R. K. Scott, *Interest Group Politics in America* (Englewood Cliffs, N.J.: Prentice-Hall, 1982), pp. 129-170.

21. See, for instance, N. H. Halperin, *Bureaucratic Politics and Foreign Policy* (Washington, D.C.: Brookings Institution, 1974), p. 101. The pattern is implied in Aberbach, Putnam, and Rockman, *Bureaucrats and Politicians in Western Democracies*, pp. 94-100.

22. B. L. Barker, "A Profile of U.S. Multinational Companies in 1977," *Survey of Current Business* 61, no. 10 (October 1981): 40.

23. Kingman Brewster, Jr., *Anti-Trust and American Business Abroad* (New York: McGraw-Hill, 1958), pp. 5, 18-23.

24. See, for instance, John T. Dunlop, ed., *Business and Public Policy* (Boston: Harvard University Graduate School of Business Administration, Division of Research, distributed by the Harvard University Press, 1980), p. 1.

25. A. T. Demaree, "Aramco Is a Lesson in the Management of Chaos," *Fortune* 89, no. 2 (February 1974): 58-65. The ultimate effect of Aramco's response was greatly mitigated by the fact that its partners provided substitute supplies from non-Saudi sources.

26. E. R. May, *Imperial Democracy: The Emergence of America as a Great Power* (New York: Harcourt Brace, 1961), p. 8; F. R. Dulles, *Prelude to World Power: American Diplomatic History, 1800-1900* (New York: Macmillan, 1965), pp. 136-137.

27. For background on this period and the U.S. reaction, see J. A. De Novo, "The Movement for an Aggressive Oil Policy Abroad," *American Historical Review* 61, no. 4 (July 1956): 854-876; G. D. Nash, *United States Oil Policy, 1890-1964* (Pittsburgh: University of Pittsburgh Press, 1968), pp. 49-71; and Lorenzo Meyer, *Mexico and the United States in the Oil Controversy, 1917-1942* (Austin: University of Texas Press, 1977; orig. pub. in Spanish, 1971), pp. 55-126.

28. P. W. Bidwell, *Raw Materials: A Study of American Policy* (New York: Council on Foreign Relations, 1958), p. 310.

29. M. I. Goldman, *The Enigma of Soviet Petroleum* (London: Allen and Unwin, 1980), p. 22.

30. John M. Blair, *The Control of Oil* (New York: Pantheon, 1976), pp. 54-71.

31. See, for instance, N. E. Nordhauser, *The Quest for Stability: Domestic Oil Regulation, 1917-1935* (New York: Garland, 1979), pp. 37-46.

32. The interplay between the multinational oil firms and the domestic oil producers from 1929 to 1933 is described in detail in Nordhauser, *The Quest for Stability*, pp. 47-95.

33. For background on this era, see Irvine H. Anderson, Jr., *Aramco, the United States and Saudi Arabia* (Princeton: Princeton University Press, 1981), pp. 99-106; Nash, *United States Oil Policy 1890-1964*, pp. 172-175.

34. G. W. Stocking, *Middle East Oil: A Study in Political and Economic Controversy* (Nashville: Vanderbilt University Press, 1970), p. 99.

35. This period is especially well covered in a number of studies, including C. D. Goodwin, ed., *Energy Policy in Perspective: Today's Problems, Yesterday's Solutions* (Washington, D.C.: Brookings Institution, 1981), pp. 63–83; and Anderson, *Aramco, the United States and Saudi Arabia*, pp. 35–107. See also Herbert Feis, *Seen from E.A.: Three International Episodes* (New York: Knopf, 1947), pp. 156–170.

36. Federal Trade Commission, *The International Petroleum Cartel* (Washington, D.C.: Government Printing Office, 1952).

37. B. I. Kaufmann, *The Oil Cartel Case* (Westport, Conn.: Greenwood Press, 1978), pp. 28–33.

38. Carl Solberg, *Oil Power* (New York: Mason Charter, 1976), p. 180.

39. President's Materials Policy Commission, *Resources for Freedom*, 5 vols. (Washington, D.C.: Government Printing Office, 1952).

40. See, for instance, D. R. Bohi and Milton Russell, *Limiting Oil Imports: An Economic History and Analysis* (Baltimore: John Hopkins University Press, 1978); E. A. Copp, *Regulating Competition in Oil: Governmental Intervention in the U.S. Refining Industry, 1948–1975* (College Station, Tex.: Texas A&M University Press, 1976).

41. The marginal cost to the companies of Saudi Arabian oil at the time was estimated at 30 cents per barrel, while the market price was $1.75. See M. A. Adelman, *The World Petroleum Market* (Baltimore: Johns Hopkins University Press, 1972), p. 145.

42. Bohi and Russell, *Limiting Oil Imports*, pp. 144–187; Goodwin, *Energy Policy in Perspective*, pp. 251–261.

43. Cabinet Task Force on Oil Import Control, *The Oil Import Question: A Report on the Relationship of Oil Imports to the National Security* (Washington, D.C.: Government Printing Office, 1970), p. 75; Copp, *Regulating Competition in Oil*, p. 103.

44. See Raymond Vernon, ed., *The Oil Crisis* (New York: Norton, 1976), pp. 3–7.

45. The episode is explored in U.S. Senate, Committee on Foreign Relations, Subcommittee on Multinational Corporations, *Multinational Corporations and U.S. Foreign Policy: Hearings*, Part 5, 93rd Cong., 1st Sess., 1973. It is well summarized in S. D. Krasner, *Defending the National Interest: Raw Materials Investments and U.S. Foreign Policy* (Princeton: Princeton University Press, 1978), pp. 262–265.

46. See, for instance, Robert B. Stobaugh and Daniel Yergin, eds., *Energy Future* (New York: Random House, 1979); and David A. Deese and Joseph S. Nye, eds., *Energy and Security* (Cambridge, Mass.: Ballinger, 1981). *Energy Future* focuses on the long-run vulnerability associated with dependence on nonrenewable resources and imported oil as major energy sources. *Energy and Security* is concerned with the implications of a drastic reduction in crude oil from foreign sources as a result of either a "bargained extortion" or "chaotic interruption."

47. For a discussion of the institutional factors — including the role of private oil companies — in IEA program implementation, see Robert O. Keohane,

"The International Energy Agency: State Influence and Transgovernmental Politics," *International Organization* 32, no. 4 (Autumn 1978): 929–951. For a more detailed analysis of the IEA's institutions and legal arrangements, see Richard Scott, "Innovation in International Organization: The International Energy Agency," *Hasting International and Comparative Law Review*, Inaugural Issues (Spring 1977): 1–56.

48. For instance, Goodwin, *Energy Policy in Perspective*, pp. 547–600.

49. In a poll taken in December 1973, 25 percent of the respondents ascribed the oil crisis to the oil companies themselves and 42 percent to the federal government. Reported in Vernon, *The Oil Crisis*, p. 85.

50. "Watt Announces Final Approval of Big Offshore Oil-Leasing Plan," *New York Times*, July 22, 1982, p. A18. See also P.S. Basile, "U.S. Energy Policy," in W. L. Kohl, ed., *After the Second Oil Crisis* (Lexington, Mass.: D. C. Heath, 1982), p. 221.

51. See, for instance, Joseph Brandes, *Herbert Hoover and Economic Diplomacy* (Pittsburgh: University of Pittsburgh Press, 1962), p. 110.

52. Relevant portions of the committee's conclusions are found in Temporary National Economic Committee, *Final Report and Recommendations* (Washington, D.C.: Government Printing Office, 1941); and idem, *Competition and Monopoly in American Industry* (Washington, D.C.: Government Printing Office, 1940).

53. Principal adjudicated cases were *U.S.* v. *National Lead Co.*, 63 F Supp. 513 (SDNY 1945), affmd, 332 US 319 (1947); and *U.S.* v. *Aluminum Co. of America*, 148 F20 416 (2nd Cir. 1945); and *U.S.* v. *General Electric Co.*, 80 F Supp. 989 (SDNY 1948). See James R. Atwood and Kingman Brewster, *Antitrust and American Business Abroad*, 2nd ed. (Colorado Springs: Shepard's/McGraw-Hill, 1981), pp. 32–34.

54. Marian Radetzki and Stephen Zorn, *Financing Mining Projects in Developing Countries* (London: Mining Journal Books, 1979), pp. 87–98.

55. On the reactive policies of the Overseas Private Investment Corporation, see Charles Lipson, "The Development of Expropriation Insurance: The Role of Corporate Preferences and State Initiatives," *International Organization* 32, no. 2 (Spring 1978): 351–375.

56. Commission on Foreign Economic Policy, *Report to the President and the Congress* (Washington, D.C.: Government Printing Office, 1954, pp. 39–41.

57. National Commission on Materials Policy, *Material Needs and the Environment Today and Tomorrow: Final Report* (Washington, D.C.: Government Printing Office, 1974), pp. 9–24 to 9–26.

58. See, for instance, *Havana Charter for an International Trade Organization*, March 24, 1948, Dept. of State Publication 3206 (Washington, D.C.: Government Printing Office, 1948), ch. 6.

59. See A. E. Eckes, Jr., *The United States and the Global Struggle for Minerals* (Austin: University of Texas Press, 1979), p. 225.

60. One of the quixotic exceptions was Henry Kissinger's proposal, in his role as secretary of state, for a common fund to stabilize a number of different com-

modities. Ultimately, the proposal was whittled down to insignificant proportions and adopted. See Eckes, *The United States and the Global Struggle for Minerals*, pp. 253–254; also U.S. Department of State, *Bulletin*, no. 74 (May 31, 1976): 657–672.

61. "Law of the Sea," *New York Times*, April 8, 1982, p. D1.

62. See, for instance, C. F. Bergsten, "The Threat from the Third World," *Foreign Policy* 11 (Summer 1973): 102–124. Also Zuhayr Mikdashi, "Collusion Could Work," *Foreign Policy* 14 (Spring 1974): 57–67.

63. See Eckes, *The United States and the Global Struggle for Minerals*, pp. 244–255.

64. Ibid., p. 38.

65. Ibid., pp. 140–141.

66. Ibid., pp. 169–170.

67. Reported in U.S. Senate, Committee on Armed Services, *Inquiry into the Strategic and Critical Material Stockpiles of the United States: Hearings*, 87th Cong., 2nd Sess. (Washington, D.C.: Government Printing Office, pp. 1080–85.

68. Eckes, *The United States and the Global Struggle for Minerals*, p. 215.

69. Ibid., p. 214.

70. Ibid., p. 222.

71. National Commission on Materials Policy, *Material Needs and the Environment Today and Tomorrow*.

72. National Commission on Supplies and Shortages, *The Commodity Shortages of 1973–1974: Case Studies* (Washington, D.C.: Government Printing Office, 1976); and idem, *Government and the Nation's Resources* (Washington, D.C.: Government Printing Office, December 1976).

73. Charles River Associates, "Public and Private Stockpiling for Future Shortages" (Cambridge, Mass., 1976).

74. "Jamaica: Half a Cheer," *The Economist*, January 23, 1982, p. 46; "Reagan Jamaican Push Helps U.S. Industry," *New York Times*, April 28, 1982, pp. A1 and D4.

75. Krasner, *Defending the National Interest*, is a particularly apposite study, concentrating on U.S. policies toward foreign direct investment in the raw materials field.

5. Japan's Institutions and Practices

1. T. J. Pempel, "Japanese Foreign Economic Policy," in P. J. Katzenstein, ed., *Between Power and Plenty* (Madison: University of Wisconsin Press, 1978), pp. 139–190; Hugh Patrick and Henry Rosovsky, eds., *Asia's New Giant* (Washington, D.C.: Brookings Institution, 1976); E. F. Denison and W. K. Chung, *How Japan's Economy Grew So Fast: The Sources of Postwar Expansion* (Washington, D.C.: Brookings Institution, 1976); Herman Kahn, *The Emerging Japanese Superstate* (Englewood Cliffs, N.J.: Prentice-Hall, 1970); G. C. Allen, *Japan's Economic Policy* (New York: Holmes and Meier, 1980); Jiro Yao, ed., *Monetary Factors in Japanese Economic Growth* (Kobe, Japan: Research Institute for Economics and Business Administration, Kobe University, 1979); James

Abegglen, ed., *Business Strategies for Japan* (Tokyo: Sophia University, 1970); Kazushi Ohkawa and Miyohei Shinohara, eds., *Patterns of Japanese Economic Development: A Quantitative Appraisal* (New Haven: Yale University Press, 1979); Richard Caves and Masu Uekusa, *Industrial Organization in Japan* (Washington, D.C.: Brookings Institution, 1976); Kazushi Ohkawa and Henry Rosovsky, *Japanese Growth: Trend Acceleration in the Twentieth Century* (Stanford: Stanford University Press, 1973); Wilbur Monro and Eisuke Sakakibara, *The Japanese Industrial Society: Its Organizational, Cultural, and Economic Underpinnings* (Austin: Bureau of Business Research, University of Texas at Austin, 1977); Ezra Vogel, *Japan as Number One: Lessons for America* (Cambridge, Mass.: Harvard University Press, 1979).

2. For information concerning Japanese politics in general, and the anatomy of the Liberal Democratic Party in particular, see Edwin O. Reischauer, *The Japanese* (Cambridge, Mass.: Harvard University Press, 1977), pp. 234–331. See also Hans Baerwald, "Parties, Factions, and the Diet," in Murakami Hyoe and Johannes Hirschmeier, eds., *Politics and Economics in Contemporary Japan* (Tokyo: Japan Culture Institute, 1979), pp. 21–63: and I. M. Destler et al., *Managing an Alliance: The Politics of U.S.–Japanese Relations* (Washington, D.C.: Brookings Institution, 1976), pp. 49–60.

3. Sueyoshi Ohtani, *Who Is to Be Tried* (Los Angeles: ITS Information Co., 1978), p. 227; Reischauer, *The Japanese*, pp. 263–265.

4. See M. Y. Yoshino, *The Japanese Marketing System* (Cambridge, Mass.: MIT Press, 1971), pp. 131–137. Yoshino, who is thoroughly familiar with both U.S. and Japanese merchandising methods, is presently of the view that Japanese distributors resort to price competition more readily than their U.S. counterparts.

5. For information reflecting the importance of advertising in Japan, see Toshio Naito, "How Advertising Works in Japan: The Market and the People," *Dentsu's Japan Marketing/Advertising*, no. 14 (January 1979): 40.

6. On bankruptcies, see, for instance, MITI, Chusho Kigyo Hakusho (Tokyo, 1980), pp. 53–57.

7. Caves and Uekusa, *Industrial Organization in Japan*, pp. 47–87, 141–154; Vogel, *Japan as Number One*, pp. 65–84; Abegglen, *Business Strategies for Japan*, pp. 71–82; and Eugene Kaplan, *Japan: The Government–Business Relationship* (Washington, D.C.: Department of Commerce, 1972).

8. For a general description of administrative guidance and its use in Japan, see Gardner Ackley and Hiromitsu Ishi, "Fiscal, Monetary, and Related Policies," in Patrick and Rosovsky, eds., *Asia's New Giant*, pp. 236–239; and Vogel, *Japan as Number One*, pp. 75–76.

9. *Petroleum Intelligence Weekly* 18, no. 35 (August 27, 1979): 4; ibid. 18, no. 52 (December 24, 1979): 7; "Costly Spot Oil 'Shopping' Is Going to Be Penalized," *Japan Economic Journal*, December 4, 1979, p. 1; and "Gov't Will Curb Buying of High-Priced Iranian Oil," ibid., December 18, 1979, p. 1.

10. "Pessimism Strengthens over Iran Petrochemical Project," *Japan Economic Journal*, September 8, 1981, p. 16; Martha Ann Caldwell, "The Dilemma of Japan's Oil Dependency," in R. A. Morse, ed., *The Politics of Japan's Energy Strategy* (Berkeley: University of California Press, 1981), pp. 72–74.

11. See Taketsugu Tsurutani, *Political Change in Japan: Response to Postindustrial Challenge* (New York: D. McKay, 1977), p. 27; also Ryutaro Komiya and Kozo Yamamoto, "Japan: The Officer in Charge of Economic Affairs," *History of Political Economy* 13, no. 3 (Fall 1981): 600–628.

12. See, for instance, Vogel, *Japan as Number One*, pp. 36–40, 60–61; Albert Craig, "Functional and Dysfunctional Aspects of Government Bureaucracy," in E. F. Vogel, ed., *Modern Japanese Organization and Decision-Making* (Berkeley: University of California Press, 1975), pp. 20–28; and Tracy Dahlby, "Anatomy of Japan, Part One: The Bureaucrats," *Far Eastern Economic Review* 111, no. 13 (March 20, 1981): 34–40.

13. Reischauer, *The Japanese*, pp. 286–297; Kanji Haitani, *The Japanese Economic System: An Institutional Overview* (Lexington, Mass.: D. C. Heath, 1976), pp. 87–92; Nobutaka Ike, *Japanese Politics: Patron-Client Democracy* (New York: Knopf, 1972), pp. 16–17, 72–73; Takeshi Ishida, *Japanese Society* (New York: Random House, 1971), pp. 37–40.

14. An outstanding analysis that documents both these points appears in Martha Ann Caldwell, "Petroleum Politics in Japan: State and Industry in a Changing Context," diss., University of Wisconsin, 1981, reproduced by University Microfilms, Ann Arbor, Michigan, 1982.

15. For information that brings out the conflicting nature of Japanese bureaucratic politics, see I. C. Magaziner and Thomas Hout, *Japanese Industrial Policy* (Berkeley: Policy Studies Institute, 1980), pp. 53–54; Chalmers Johnson, "MITI and Japanese International Economic Policy," in Robert Scalapino, ed., *The Foreign Policy of Modern Japan* (Berkeley: University of California Press, 1977), pp. 230–244; and Pempel, "Japanese Foreign Economic Policy," p. 155.

16. The struggle among government agencies and power companies over the shape of the Japanese nuclear power industry, for instance, reflects all these elements. See R. W. Gale, "Tokyo Electric Power Company," in Morse, *The Politics of Japan's Energy Strategy*, pp. 89–100.

17. See Rodney Clark, *The Japanese Company* (New Haven: Yale University Press, 1979), pp. 125–134; Kazuo Noda, "Big Business Organization," in Vogel, ed., *Modern Japanese Organization and Decision-Making*, pp. 120–129, 144–145; and M. Y. Yoshino, "Emerging Japanese Multinational Enterprises," ibid., pp. 158–166, Also see Thomas Rohlen, *For Harmony and Strength: Japanese White Collar Organization in Anthropological Perspective* (Berkeley: University of California Press, 1974), pp. 107–108, 114–115.

18. The connection in general is explored in Alexander Gerschenkron, *Economic Backwardness in Historical Perspective* (Cambridge, Mass.: Harvard University Press, 1962), pp. 44, 354–355, 358.

19. Ackley and Ishi, "Fiscal, Monetary, and Related Policies," pp. 202–204; Yoshio Suzuki, *Money and Banking in Contemporary Japan* (New Haven: Yale University Press, 1980), p. 166.

20. Japan Economic Institute, *JEI Report*, October 9, 1981.

21. Translated into English from *Mining Handbook*, 1978 and 1980 editions, published in 1979 and 1981 respectively in Tokyo by the Japan Agency for

Natural Resources and Development, and reproduced in Economic Consulting Services, "Nonfuel Mineral Policies of Six Industrialized Countries: Final Report" (Washington, D.C., September 1981; prepared for the U.S. Department of Commerce), Table VI-20.

22. See, for instance, Gerald Curtis, "Big Business and Political Influence," in Vogel, ed., *Modern Japanese Organization and Decision-Making*, pp. 33–70; and Tracy Dahlby, "Anatomy of Japan, Part Three: The Businessmen," in *Far Eastern Economic Review* 112, no. 18 (April 24, 1981): 76–80.

23. For a summary of some major reports of this kind bearing on energy policy, see Akira Mastuzawa and Akinobu Tsumura, "Evolution of Japanese Energy Policy," *Journal of Petroleum Technology* 32, no. 10 (October 1980): 1691–94.

24. Magaziner and Hout, *Japanese Industrial Policy*, p. 38.

25. Quoted in "Japanese Adjust to Oil Supply Changes," *Oil and Gas Journal*, January 26, 1981, p. 96.

26. Chalmers Johnson, *Japan's Public Policy Companies* (Washington, D.C.: American Enterprise Institute, 1978), pp. 25–60.

27. Haitani, *The Japanese Economic System*, pp. 156–158; "Japan's Gentle Persuaders," *The Economist*, January 17–23, 1981, pp. 70–71; Eisuke Sakakibara, Robert Feldman, and Yuzo Harada, "Japanese Financial System in Comparative Perspective," U.S.-Japan Program, Center for International Affairs, Harvard University, 1981, pp. 52–61.

28. One of the best accounts of the period up to World War II is contained in I. H. Anderson, Jr., *The Standard-Vacuum Oil Company and United States East Asian Policy, 1933–1941* (Princeton: Princeton University Press, 1975). The source includes an exhaustive bibliography.

29. Anderson, *The Standard-Vacuum Oil Company*, p. 64.

30. Asado Sadao, "The Japanese Navy and the United States," in Dorothy Borg and Shumpei Okatomo, eds., *Pearl Harbor as History: Japanese-American Relations, 1931–1941* (New York: Columbia University Press, 1973), p. 237.

31. Compare Anderson, *The Standard-Vacuum Oil Company*, p. 57.

32. Ibid., p. 62.

33. Ibid., pp. 171–192.

34. J. B. Cohen, *Japan's Economy in War and Reconstruction* (Minneapolis: University of Minnesota Press, 1949), p. 140.

35. Yoshi Tsurumi, "Japan," in Raymond Vernon, ed., *The Oil Crisis* (New York: Norton, 1976), p. 115; Caldwell, "Petroleum Politics in Japan," p. 43.

36. Caldwell, "Petroleum Politics in Japan," p. 49.

37. The various sources disagree somewhat on the precise amount under foreign control, perhaps because of definitional problems; the lowest estimate is 50 percent, the highest 75 percent. The sources include Tosuke Iguchi Gendai Nihon Sangyo Hattatsushi [Developmental History of Modern Japanese Industry], vol. 2 (Tokyo: Gendai Nihon Sangyo Hattatsushi, 1964), p. 464; "Japan's Import Rules Trim Majors' Markets," *Oil and Gas Journal* 58, no. 30 (July 25, 1960); "Kurusania genyu kyokyu," *Nihon Keizai Shinbun*, March 25, 1960, p. 4.

38. "Do naru yokkaichi mondai," *Ekonomisuto*, May 1, 1952, p. 10.

39. See "Japan's Big Independent Planning to Double Everything," *Oil and Gas Journal*, Oct. 17, 1960, p. 82; Tosuke Iguchi, *Sekiyu*, vol. 2 of Gendai

Nihon Sangyo Hattatsushi, p. 464; Japan's Import Rules Trim Majors' Markets," *Oil and Gas Journal*, July 25, 1960, p. 141; and "Kurusania genyu kyokyu, karutekkusu, gogatsu tsumi kara nisseki ni," *Nihon Keizai Shinbun*, March 25, 1960, p. 4.

40. "Nanasha ga chosadan o haken: Indoneshia yuden kaihatsu," *Nihon Keizai Shinbun*, September 14, 1958, p. 3; "8Oman Ton Ijo no 40% o Nihon e . . . . ," ibid., October 7, 1959, p. 3; "Gutaika no dankai ni hairu: Kitasumatora yuden kaihatsu," ibid., October 16, 1959, p. 4.

41. Tosuke Iguchi, *Sekiyu* (Tokyo: Gendai Nihon Sangyo Hattatsushi Kenkyukai, 1964), p. 509.

42. "Gaishi shakkan ni ittei kijun," *Nihon Keizai Shinbun*, March 13, 1962, p. 4.

43. Yoshi Tsurumi, "Japan," in Vernon, ed., *The Oil Crisis*, p. 115.

44. "Gaishi shakkan ni ittei kijun," *Nihon Keizai Shinbun*, March 13, 1962, p. 4.

45. "Seisei ote: Sekiyu gyohoan ni hantai . . . ," *Nihon Keizai Shinbun*, August 25, 1961; "Enerugii seisaku no arikata: Denryoku gyokai ga toitsu kenkai . . . ," ibid., December 20, 1961, p. 4; "Sekiyu gyoho ni hantai: Tekko gyokai . . . ," ibid., January 28, 1962, p. 4; "Sekiyu gyohoan ni sansei: Sekiyu kogyoren rijikai . . . ," ibid., January 19, 1962, p. 4.

46. See "Sekiyu gyoho," in *Tsushosangyo Roppo* (Tokyo, published annually), Law 128, May 2, 1962; "New Japanese Oil Law Stirs Uneasiness," *Oil and Gas Journal*, June 25, 1962, p. 92.

47. "Daikyo sekiyu: Genyu shori o zenmen teishi . . . ," *Nihon Keizai Shinbun*, September 29, 1963, p. 4; "Idemitsu kosan, tsuyoi fuman; Shacho dan," ibid., October 5, 1963, p. 4; Idemitsu, keiei ohaba ni akka," ibid., October 6, 1963, p. 5; "Muhai seishiki kettei: Idemitsu kosan," ibid., October 26, 1963, p. 5; "Kaki seisan chosei tsuzukeru, sekiyu renmei kinkyuri . . . ," ibid., December 4, 1963, p. 4; "'Idemitsu taisaku' shincho ni, sekiyu renmei . . . ," ibid., December 6, 1963, p. 5; "Settoku ni ojinai, idemitsu shacho wa kataru," ibid., December 12, 1963, p. 5; "Japanese Juggle Refinery Runs Formula," *Oil and Gas Journal*, March 9, 1964, p. 64; "Idemitsu mondai kaketsu no kizashi, konshuchu ni assenan," *Nihon Keizai Shinbun*, January 19, 1964, p. 5; "Idemitsu mondai ga kaiketsu, tsusansho assenan o ryosho," ibid., January 25, evening, 1964, p. 1; "Zosetsubun chosei ni shinkijun, tsusansho, hatsugenken tsuyomeru," ibid., January 26, 1964, p. 3.

48. Caldwell, "Petroleum Politics in Japan," p. 123.

49. Robert B. Stobaugh, "The Oil Companies in the Crisis," in Vernon, ed., *The Oil Crisis*, pp. 192–193.

50. R. A. Morse, "Energy and Japan's National Security Strategy," in Morse, *The Politics of Japan's Energy Strategy*, p. 40.

51. See, for instance, Agency of Natural Resources and Energy, *Energy in Japan: Facts and Figures* (Tokyo: Ministry of International Trade and Industry, 1980), pp. 18–24; *The Vision of MITI Policies in 1980s* (Tokyo: Ministry of International Trade and Industry, 1980), pp. 11–13; *White Paper on the International Trade* (Tokyo: Ministry of International Trade and Industry, 1980), pp. 92–97.

52. See especially Caldwell, "Petroleum Politics in Japan," pp. 274–370.

53. Jeffrey Segal, "The Rise of the 'Sogo Shosha,'" *Petroleum Economist* 48, no. 5 (May, 1981): 201–204.

54. David Watts, "Export Drive," *November 1979 Middle East Economic Digest Special Report: Japan and the Middle East*, November 1979, p. 51; Edmund O'Sullivan, "Saudi Arabia: A Deal — Technical Expertise For Oil," *December 1980 Middle East Economic Digest Special Report: Japan and the Middle East*, December 1980, p. 63.

55. Hiroshi Yokokawa, "Japanese Oil Industry and Oil Policies," U.S.-Japan Program, Center for International Affairs, Harvard University, Working Paper, April 1982.

56. Economic Consulting Services, "Nonfuel Mineral Policies," Table IV-17.

57. Economic Consulting Services, "Nonfuel Mineral Policies," Table VI-12, derived from *Kinzaku Kogyo Jigyodan no Gaiyo* [Metal Mining Agency Overview] (Tokyo: Metal Mining Agency of Japan, 1980); Kiyohiko Nanao, "Minerals Policy in Japan," in *Mineral Society*, vol. 3 (New York: Pergamon, 1979).

58. See, for instance, Y. Okawara, "Japanese Minerals Policy: A New Dimension," *Mining Review*, October 1978 (Canberra, Australia), p. 4.

59. MITI, *White Paper on International Trade 1980* (Tokyo: September 1980), p. 94, Table 4-1.

60. By 1981 these duties had been reduced to 5–10 percent; earlier, they were much higher. *Customs Tariff Schedule of Japan, 1981* (Tokyo: Japan Tariff Association, 1981).

61. A. K. Young, *The Sogo Shosha: Japan's Multinational Trading Companies* (Boulder, Colo.: Westview Press, 1979), pp. 148–149.

62. Wolfgang Gluschke et al., *Copper: The Next Fifteen Years* (Dordrecht, Holland: D. Reidel, 1979), p. 130; also Economic Consulting Services, "Nonfuel Mineral Policies," Table VI-14.

63. Economic Consulting Services, "Nonfuel Mineral Policies," Table VI-14.

64. Lloyd's *Register of Shipping Statistical Tables*, London, various dates.

65. R. O. Goss and C. E. Jones, "The Economics of Size in Dry Bulk Carriers," in R. O. Goss, ed., *Advances in Maritime Economics* (Cambridge: Cambridge University Press, 1977), pp. 90–123, reports that overall costs per ton when shipping ore in a 120,000-ton carrier amounted to about one-third of the costs in a 15,000-ton vessel.

66. Terutomo Ozawa, "Japan's Resource Dependency and Overseas Investment," *Journal of World Trade Law* 11, no. 1 (January-February 1977): 64.

67. "Australia's Iron Boom Comes Down to Earth," *Business Week*, no. 1928 (August 13, 1966): 99–100.

68. E. Gough Whitlam, *A Pacific Community* (Cambridge, Mass.: Harvard University Press, 1981), pp. 82–83.

69. Australian Department of Trade and Resources, *Australia's Mineral Resources* (Canberra, 1980), p. 5.

70. Australia/Japan Joint Study Group on Raw Materials Processing, *Australian and Japanese Aluminum Smelting Industries: Future Development and Relationships* (Canberra: Australian Government Publishing Service, 1980), pp. 6–8.

71. Y. Okawara, "Japanese Mineral Policy," p. 4; "Japanese Electricity: The Coal Rush Continues," *The Economist*, April 22, 1981, p. 59. For Japan's acquisition practices in coal, see Joseph D'Cruz, "Quasi Integration in Raw Material Markets: The Overseas Procurement of Coking Coal by the Japanese Steel Industry," diss., Harvard Business School, 1979, esp. pp. 178–192.

72. For an official summary of Japan's stockpiling policies, see MITI, *White Paper on International Trade, 1981* (Tokyo: MITI Information Office, 1981), pp. 132–133.

73. ECS report, Table VI-16, based on data from *Mining Handbook 1980* (Tokyo: Japanese Agency for Natural Resources and Energy, 1981).

74. The program is described in "Tariff Quota May Be Used to Aid Aluminum Industry," *Japan Economic Journal*, October 13, 1981, p. 3; "Japanese Ministry's Plan to End Tariffs in Some Aluminum Draws U.S. Criticism," *Wall Street Journal*, October 1981, p. 31.

75. "Japan Brings the Curtain Down on the Stars of Yesteryear," *The Economist*, September 26, 1981, p. 67; "Natural Resource and Energy Agency Is Asked to Take Up Excessive Oil Refining," *Japan Economic Journal*, January 12, 1982, p. 6.

76. Stuart Kirby, "Japan's Role in the 1980s," Economist Intelligence Unit Report 81, London, June 1980, pp. 8, 11.

77. "Brazil's Steelnut," *The Economist*, June 12, 1982, p. 78.

6. Feeding the Giants

1. See, for example, M. A. Adelman's views reported in "U.S. Strategy to Tempt OPEC Members to Cut Oil Prices Is Urged by Professor," *New York Times*, September 15, 1975, p. 27; Milton Friedman's somewhat similar predictions for OPEC can be found in "People and Business," *New York Times*, April 23, 1975, p. 59.

2. But see the scenarios explored in H. H. Landsberg et al., *Energy: The Next Twenty Years* (Cambridge, Mass.: Ballinger, 1979), pp. 77–113.

3. A striking illustration is the projections contained in Council on Environmental Quality and Department of State, *The Global 2000 Report to the President* (no date or place; issued Washington, D.C., 1982), pp. 187–225. Following a thoughtful identification of the many imponderables in the supply and demand for oil and minerals, the report nevertheless presents point estimates for the year 2000.

4. See E. A. Deagle, Jr., Bijon Mossavar-Rahmoni, and Richard Huff, *Energy in the 1980s: An Analysis of Recent Studies* (New York: Group of Thirty, 1981), covering an analysis of fifty-three such projections.

5. *Mineral Facts and Problems*, U.S. Bureau of Mines Bulletin 667, U.S. Department of the Interior (Washington, D.C.: Government Printing Office, 1976), pp. 28–240.

6. *Mineral Facts and Problems*, p. 450.

7. See also R. W. Arad et al., *Sharing Global Resources* (New York: McGraw-Hill, 1979), pp. 40–41, 126–127.

8. For a discussion of European cutbacks in steel production, see Susan Strange, "The Management of Surplus Capacity: Or How Does Theory Stand Up to Protectionism 1970's Style?" *International Organization* 33, no. 3 (Summer 1979): 303–334.

9. For a thoughtful analysis of the factors likely to affect the location of the steel industry in the future, see Bela Gold, "Pressures for Restructuring the World Steel Industry in the 1980s: A Case Study in Challenges to Industrial Adaptation," *Quarterly Review of Economics and Business* 22, no. 1 (Spring 1982): 45–66. See also R. W. Crandall, *The U.S. Steel Industry in Recurrent Crisis* (Washington, D.C.: Brookings Institution, 1981).

10. MITI, "The Vision of MITI Policies in the 1980s," MITI Information Office, Tokyo, March 17, 1980.

11. Compare the Reagan administration's refusal to seek powers for dealing with the emergency distribution of oil in a period of shortage. "President Is Upheld on Oil Veto," *New York Times*, March 25, 1982, p. D1.

12. This possibility is raised also in Allan North, ed., *The Crisis in World Materials: A U.S.-Japan Symposium* (Newark, N.J.: Rutgers University Graduate School of Business Administration, 1974), p. 14.

13. See, for instance, "Talk of an Oil Import Fee," *New York Times*, April 8, 1982, p. D1.

14. Raymond Vernon, "Organizational and Institutional Responses to International Risk," in Richard Herring, ed., *Managing International Risk* (Cambridge: Cambridge University Press, 1983), forthcoming.

15. See Malcolm Gillis, Ricardo Godoy, and Micheline Mescher, "Fiscal, Financial, and Related Provisions in Petroleum Contracts in Fourteen Countries," Institute for International Development, Harvard University, January 24, 1982.

16. A good deal is often made of the threat implicit in cutoffs of the rarer ores, such as manganese and chrome. But the disruptive implications of these threats are as a rule exaggerated. See M. M. Kostecki, ed., *Soviet Impact on Commodity Markets* (London: Macmillan, 1983).

17. See, for instance, J. J. Kaplan, "Raw-Materials Policy: Japan and the United States," in Isaiah Frank, ed., *The Japanese Economy in International Perspective* (Baltimore: Johns Hopkins Press, 1975), pp. 231–247; also *U.S.-Japan Energy Relationship in the 1980s*, Atlantic Council Policy Papers, Washington, D.C., June 1981, pp. 43–46.

18. See, for instance, Isaac Shapiro, "The Risen Sun: Japanese Gaullism?" *Foreign Policy*, no. 41 (Winter 1980–81): 62–81. See also MITI, *White Paper on International Trade, 1981* (Tokyo, 1981), pp. 122–131.

19. For a contemporary set of proposals that follow the lines of the Paley report, see Michael Shafer, "Mineral Myths," *Foreign Policy*, no. 47 (Summer 1982): 154–171.

20. P. S. Basile, "U.S. Energy Policy," in W. L. Kohl, ed., *After the Second Oil Crisis* (Lexington, Mass.: D.C. Heath, 1982), esp. pp. 209–223, comes to a similar conclusion with respect to oil.

INDEX

Page numbers in *italic* indicate tables and figures.